thedrops

JANISMAHNURE

In The Name of Allah, The Most Merciful, Most Compassionate

Dedication

To my mother and father for their sacrifices and my freedom; my beloved Anika for her inspiration; my Sarika for her praise; and my humble secret editor.

To my teachers, Sheikh Omar Suleiman, Ustaadh Nouman Ali Khan, Ustaadh Mohammed Hannini and Ustaadh Muhammad Elshinawy.

And to my friends and followers who have been with *Drops of Knowledge* from the beginning.

Table of Contents

3

the
burden
of sin

Death isn't scary when you imagine the Angel of Death coming down with 500 angels carrying bouquets of flowers for you, smelling fragrant, greeting you with 'Assalaamu Alaikum' and tells you that your beloved Allah is waiting to meet you.

It's scary when you realize that you lived such a life that the Angel of Death may come to rip your heart from your body and stuff it in a suffocating pouch and be utterly disgusted by you.

Even a life full of "just minor sins".

— — —

"The imaan we have is more valuable than the seven heavens. And we will realize how valuable this 'la ilaha ila Allah' is, after we die." - Sheikh Muhammad Yasir

The sheikh explained how if we bought a car for $1,000, we wouldn't really care where we park it or who touches it. But if we bought a car for $100,000 we are careful with where we are parking it and who is next to it and even if one of our own family members scratched it, we would be angered.

But our imaan, our faith is more valuable than a Mercedes Benz. We should be guarding it with so much more.

And sometimes safeguarding the imaan means forcing yourself to stop watching certain shows so you don't become immune to seeing sin. Sometimes it means not going somewhere where people will be sinning incessantly or where you will be tempted to do so. Sometimes it means doing the sunnah portion of duhr even though it seems to take so long. Sometimes it means letting go of friends, going somewhere alone, perhaps even being alone for a bit before surrounding yourself with new friends, friends aware of Jannah, friends who motivate you to pray more than required. Sometimes it means sitting somewhere uncomfortable simply for the sake of knowledge and the sake of finding that imaan high.

We shouldn't accept our own excuses - you are not a lazy person, you are not too tired to pray on time, you are not too busy to read a page of Quran, you are not too poor to donate.

It's not imaan that we just believe in Allah. Believing in Allah means doing things that please Him. Believing means avoiding the things that displease Him. Believing means being aware of His wrath and His mercy.

But the shahada can't be a phrase on your lips and not in your heart.

Because imagine you are dying, and in your last moments, loved ones appear, people who have passed before, and they plead with you saying that Islam is the wrong religion - if the shahada was simply on your lips and not in your heart - will you be able to actually say it. Or will you be swayed by these illusions and tricks of the shaytaan.

And with that, we have to ask Allah to keep us firm in this imaan and die upon this imaan.

Ya muqallib al quluub thabbit qalbi 'ala deenik.

Oh Turner of hearts, make my heart firm upon your religion.

— — —

"Can you buy something to erase that feeling of guilt after you commit a sin." - Hassan Mohammed

Or rather, can all the money in the world fix that feeling? There's a reason that feeling is there. It's part of your innate nature. Either you repent after that feeling, or divulge in more sin to block out the feeling. And many people pick the latter. Usually turning to music or maybe smoking/drinking or maybe sex.

And if you keep ignoring the feeling, then it will eventually disappear. But that also means that either shaytaan won or your own nafs won.

So if and when you do get the feeling. Accept it. Repent for it. And stop doing it before you become immune to guilt.

— — —

This brother wrote on the board in Arabic the word: "Ar-Raheem". And then he placed a dot under the Arabic letter "ha" and it became a "jeem" which changes the word to "Ar-Rajeem".

The word Ar-Raheem refers to something good, to Allah and His mercy. Ar-Rajeem refers to something bad, to Shaytaan, and his banishment.

He then kept taking away the dot, and then adding it back again. On a basic level - it is just a trick, the switching of a letter to make a different word. But on a bigger, conceptual level - you can think about how easy it is for something good to become something bad. Seemingly good things can become harmful for you. Even blessings can sometimes be a test that you don't pass, essentially harming you. Your intentions can also make something good into something bad - perhaps a good deed leading you to have pride.

We need to be wary of ourselves constantly.

— — —

"At that moment, you would rather your own mother be burning in the fire in place of you." - Sheikh Waleed Basyouni

[This is in reference to Surah Al-Ma'arij Verses 11-16]

We think that we could handle Hell. That we'll deal with our few days/decades of punishment for the sins we've committed. That it won't be too bad since we'll get Jannah eventually.

But can you imagine being in such a state that you would rather let your mother, your siblings, your children - you would trade everyone on earth to face that punishment - just to get yourself out.

The place with valleys of boiling pus, blood, fat burnt off the skin of other humans, crushed bones, all made into a liquid for you to drink. The place with chains - shackling the inhabitants of Hell because the fire pushes the bodies up as it's engulfing them and the chains are to get them back down to the pit. Fed to you fruits shaped like the heads of devils. Seeing the people next to you - the people you followed - the ones you disobeyed Allah for.

You'll be begging to get out, begging for another chance, not remembering anything you enjoyed in the dunya.

But you have the time now. To beg not to be put there.

To fast on a random day simply for the sake of Allah - and Allah pushes the Hellfire seventy years further away from your face. [Muslim]

To pray four rakats before duhr and four rakats after so Allah makes you prohibited for the Fire. [Tirmidhi]

To read Surah Al-Mulk so it intercedes for you. [Tirmidhi & Abu Dawud]

To love Allah, to fear Allah, and to have hope in Allah.

— — —

"We mess with fitnah and think: that'll never happen to me. Who are you? Are you better than Yusuf AS.?" - Sh. Muhamad ibn Faqih

This is for the one's who go close to things they know is wrong - but feel that they themselves will never commit it.

You'd be surprised to hear the stories - of the "religious" people who strayed a bit. When Allah told Adam, don't even go near the tree, it wasn't that the dirt near the tree was haraam. It was eating the fruit of the tree that was the sin. But Allah knows that going near it would eventually lead to it.

So get away from the friends you know could potentially lead you somewhere bad - the potheads, the clubbers. Stop tempting shaytaan, you are not invincible.

You can say you're not addicted to music, but does your phone have more music or more Quran. How many lines of lyrics do you hear a day and how many verses of Allah's book do you hear a day?

You boys can say that the girls are like sisters and you'll never see them in another light, and you girls can say that you're just like one of the guys, so you're cool with the boys, you'd never be interested in marrying them anyway. You can say it's just studying, you can say it's just coffee, you can say, but everyone's friends with them. You can say it's just snapchat, just instagram, it's just liking a picture - it's not zina.

It's not. But what justification are you going to spout at Allah when you're standing in front of Him. Are you going to tell Allah, "I didn't commit zina, we were just friends." Are you going to tell Him it was just a hug, just a handshake. Are you going to say that it was society's fault.

Why tempt yourself, why bother standing so close to the line separating haraam and halal, letting shaytaan twirl around you hoping you'll step over the line, blurring it on your way back.

It doesn't need to be a sin for you to stay away from it.

And if you've already crossed the line, "O My servants who have transgressed against themselves [by sinning], do not despair of the mercy of Allah. Indeed, Allah forgives all sins." (Surah Az-Zumar).

The very fact that you're reading this means Allah knows you're seeking forgiveness. So fast on the blessed day of Arafat which forgives the sins of the past year, and learn to forgive yourself.

There's no turning back to the old you. There is only one way to go from here - and that it is up, towards Allah, towards becoming a resident of Jannah.

— — —

"Shaytaan has lost all hope that he will ever be able to lead you astray in your major actions, so beware of following him in your minor actions."

A lot of us fall into this trap. We feel that because we aren't committing major sins - then we are safe. We aren't worshiping a different God, nor are we murdering or stealing or committing zina.

But what are we doing? Shaytaan is coming at us, helping us make piles of little sins - which are a big deal because us belittling our sin means that we don't think Allah's wrath is a big deal, or it means that we are arrogant in our perception of Allah's mercy.

What small sins? Like maybe not lowering our gaze when walking down the street (this includes the girls who look at the boys as well). Like cursing. Like ignoring a parent's phone call. Like white lies and cheating on exams. Like gossiping. Like watching inappropriateness (which isn't limited to pornography, but also just the "normal" intimacy in tv shows and movies)

It's all so normalized, so widespread, that the people who DON'T partake in this culture are seen as weird.

The weirdos who don't listen to music, who don't attend mixed weddings, who don't wear make-up, who don't do hookah, who don't watch movies or tv, who don't hang in coed groups, who think kissing scenes are rated-R. The ones who wear "oppressive" clothing, the boys with the pants above their ankles, and the girls wearing niqaab.

But hey, "this religion came as something strange, and will leave as something strange, so glad tiding to the stranger."

— — —

"I advise you to be shy of Allāh like you are shy of a pious man from amongst your people." - Tabarani

Honestly, the truth behind this.

People in relationships, hiding from the MSA. People hiding their history from the more "religious" people. Not snapchatting hookah because you have certain practicing friends on snapchat. Making sure no one posts pictures of you from that innappropriate event you went to. Instagramming food from your date but making sure the person you're with isn't in the picture.

You know, some people will "be themselves" and do whatever in front of whomever. But overall, it's kind of this awkward shyness.

Like it doesn't matter if they're not judging you - you still feel strange doing something remotely wrong near them.

Especially if they're actually pious - like really practicing, modest, nonjudgemental, sweet type. Then it's like you really don't want to be bad around them.

But we're always in the presence of Allah.

There was a story about a thief - someone says that a thief stealing is a sin. But a thief becoming scared while he's stealing because he hears the people of the home awakening, becomes an even greater sin.

Because that fear is the fear of the people. It places people in a higher level than Allah, audhobillah. You're not scared that Allah will punish you but you're scared that people will catch you.

Being shy with Allah means don't commit those sins that you wouldn't commit in front of others. Allah's always there. In your bedroom at 2AM as you're searching a site you shouldn't search or watching a movie that might be problematic or talking to someone in a manner you shouldn't.

And the lines aren't really blurry. That's a misconception because shaytaan makes your blur them. You know very well what is right and what is wrong. You don't need to be knowledgeable in fiqh or aqeedah or anything at all.

Sins are beautified but they feel wrong eventually. You're going against your own soul. Your fitrah. Your natural spirit knows what is right and what is wrong and it feels the guilt and disgusting nature of sins afterwards.

And if Allah watching over you is not scary enough, at least remember the angels that are writing. Even when they don't want to write it down. They must.

So let them write gleefully. Let them scribble with energy and excitement and happiness as you fill your day with the words of Allah, with duas for yourself and others, with the remembrance of Him and His messenger, and productivity throughout.

Give them good things to write on the scrolls. Don't give them sins to witness against you on the Day of Judgement. The justifications won't be there. Your own limbs will testify against you.

— — —

"You will die the way you lived. & You will be raised the way you died."

So how exactly do we want to be raised on the Day of Judgement?

How do we want the angel of death coming to us?

If the angel of death comes with a flock of angels of mercy, will they come to you if you're dying in the state of a sin?

Do we want to meet the Lord, the Most Merciful, the Giver of Gifts, the Bestower, whilst in the state of doing something wrong? Watching something we shouldn't be watching, dressed in a manner we shouldn't be dressing, talking in a way we shouldn't be talking.

Or would you rather have your loved ones with you, holding your hand, saying the shahada, seeing a glimpse of that home in Jannah. Knowing you will see their faces there too.

When you meet your beloved Allah, what state do you want to meet Him in?

Wake up before it's too late, change before that moment comes.

— — —

"When I am not willing to give up on a sin for the sake of Allah and I insist upon that sin - there is a form of polytheism there. If you're addicted to a sin - your love for Allah is not great enough to give up that sin." – Sheikh Omar Suleiman

Whether it be a big sin or a small sin - we all have sins we continuously do. Perhaps it has become second nature for us to watch something shameless (and this isn't limited to pornography, it includes things like western shows with nudity and unfortunately much of bollywood too). Perhaps it's missing prayers intentionally because "I'll just make it up later at night." Or maybe it's a relationship we justify even though deep inside, we know very well that Allah is angered by our transgression. Or lying, to our parents, to our employers, to our professors.

And we so easily justify these things - sometimes it's just the environment, the friend circle, the cultural norms, the non-practicing family members, the circumstances.

But, "That which is haram will always be haram, even if the whole world engages in it."

And our love for Allah should surpass everything. We shouldn't justify the sins, we don't need to do any of these sins - Allah is the provider, Allah is the master, Allah is the source of all happiness. So what are you really chasing?

———

"Ibraheem A.S, when Allah makes a tiny request 'How about you go to the dessert and leave your family there?' He's not gonna say 'I love everything about Islam except this whole leaving my family alone in the desert.' When Allah says jump into the fire, he didn't say 'I love Islam but this whole burning myself doesn't seem so cool' and what about when Allah says to sacrifice his son, does Ibraheem say 'Can you give a logical explanation, the social benefits of why I should do this?'" [Paraphrased from Ustaadh Nouman Ali Khan]

I never ever thought of hijab in this manner. It's always been - oh women are a treasure, oh we are saving ourselves for our husband, oh we want someone who loves us and not our body. But here we're taking a step back - the FUNDAMENTAL element of Islam is submitting to God. Allah tells us to wear hijab. So how do we disobey Him while we live on the earth that He created, eating the food the He provided. All the secondary reasons are rationales and explanations we created. The real reason is just that, we submit to Allah, we hear and we obey.

———

"If you wear hijab like those other hijab wearing girls. You'll be raised with them on the day of judgement. Not with Khadija. Not with Aisha."

This isn't a reminder for the sisters. It's also a reminder for you brothers. The ones who think short shorts for basketball are okay and muscle t-shirts in Instagram photos of your biceps don't break the rules of hayaa. Reality check. They do.

Who do you want to be? There was a poem once about what would you do if the Prophet came to your house. What would you hide? How would you dress?

Everyone knows the rules of hijab. And you know very well if you're abiding by them or breaking them. And you also know what your intentions are. You are the only one who knows your struggle, your story. And Allah knows your deepest thoughts. And yes, it's a decision you make every single day of your life.

You guys were made for Jannah. Be the people to whom the Angels of Paradise will smile at as you walk through to your palace. And if that means wearing a bit more clothes and acting a bit more modestly, then so be it. For the fire of hell is hotter.

— — —

"Allah is telling us that He will make the high path of good easy for him. The one who takes the wrong way, Allah will make the most difficult of things (of evil) - easy for him." -- excerpt from Tafseer of Surah Al-Layl from Ustaadh Nouman Ali Khan

The entire tafseer explains this in even more details but just to reflect on your own life - think about it.

When you start doing "bad", little by little, inch by inch, it just becomes so easy to continue doing the bad. Like tv: we watch a little, and then we watch a lot, and then we watch shows that we wouldn't watch with our parents around, and well, our level of hayaa and what we think is "bad" becomes skewed. Immune to other people's immodesty. It becomes easy to pause the bad tv show - pray - and then come back to it.

Small things leading to bigger things - it's so easy to sin, and continue sinning, that it becomes difficult to see the person you once were or one day aspire to be. It seems like the proper thing - is the strange thing - "you get awkward around the opposite gender, you're so weird. you don't watch this show - why not?"

And on the flip side - once you go into good, you can't leave. The small sins feel tremendous. The few minutes wasted on not worshiping Allah, makes you feel guilty. Not praying sunnah or nafl makes you feel disloyal to the Lord. Allah gives you more blessings in your wealth and in your time.

Good becomes the easiest thing for you to do. All you have to do is start it.

— — —

Kids are unbelievably impressionable.

My young girl-cousin asked if having a boy's picture on your phone is sinful. Now, I'm like .. hmm.. it's not necessarily, but then it could be bad if you keep looking at the boy's picture because we are told to lower our gaze. I wasn't going to tell her what was wrong and what was right because I want her to decide it for herself after seeing different understandings.

But then she remarked: so why did you have a picture of a boy?

And I was kind of shocked, and my brain ran through all the pics on my phone and then it hit me - I had a picture of Captain Hook from the show "Once Upon A Time". It was a long while ago, but my cousin remembered it. Now, I'm not really that celebrity following kind, I don't even know the name of the real actor that plays the character, I simply thought nothing of it - just as I used to have tons of pictures of Harry Potter when I was younger.

But then I realized how it gave the wrong message to them.

Lowering the gaze is something all of us have trouble with.

I'm sorry society has made it into a phrase only directed at you brothers. That's not how Allah intended it to be - the ayahs come one after another, tell the believing men to lower their gaze .. and then tell the believing women to lower their gaze ...

But I feel like us sisters, we have to admit that we don't try; that we feel excused, because we aren't "lusting" after the men. It's just "looking" to us.

You see a beard and it's an automatic double glance. You don't even feel bad about it.

Sisters fawning over speakers, giggling when a brother walks by, calling boys "BAE", it's not actually funny. You should hold yourself to a higher standard, to have a certain level of dignity that Allah gave you. Why decrease it for society's norms?

I don't know where the line is - with celebrities, instagram models, and speakers. But I think all of us can take a step back and contemplate - what is being written down on the right side, and what on the left.

15

And then taking into consideration the younger members of our family. When we sin - and we do it openly with our family members, we're normalizing situations, normalizing sins. So even when we grow up and eventually change our ways (as we all say, one day we'll change, one day we'll stop) - the younger ones will get confused. How come the change? Why isn't it okay? But YOU did it.

And it's hard to explain to a pre-teen why you did something that isn't totally okay with Allah.

Now imagine standing in front of Allah.

Now imagine explaining your sin to Him.

— — —

"And when the pages are made public" - from Surah At-Takwir

When friends dig back through your facebook and find something embarrassing and bump it so it appears on people's newsfeed, it's funny, and yet, terrifying at the same time. We were once like this at some point. Now, hopefully we all have clean facebooks, pages where we can potentially add our mother and nothing would disappoint her. But what about the conversations ...

What conversations would you keep and which ones would you delete. And I don't mean only the conversations with the opposite gender - but also those with our friends in which we gossiped, cursed, lied, sent things we weren't supposed to like videos or screenshots. The times we could have helped someone but chose to ignore their messages.

How about if you were to let the Prophet [saw] see. Would he be pleased with you? And he's a human being. He's not God. And this is just things on social media.

Allah sees our sins. We are shameless in showing them. We forget that the angels have to watch us commit these sins - from the small ones to the big ones. And not only must they see us - they have to write it down. And we will witness to ourselves - what exactly did we do.

And then, imagine your children doing the things you did/do.

You can clean away the history on your computer, you can delete messages and emails and photos, but the scrolls are still there until Allah wipes them clean.

So when you're asking Allah to forgive your sins - make sure to ask Him to hide them as well. To not display them so the world can see, so your parents and grandparents and friends and acquaintances and spouse and children will see.

To cover them up, to wipe them off the scrolls.

—— —— ——

"We need to make sure that our relationship with Allah is not an ugly relationship with a pretty face." - Sheikh Omar Suleiman

This is the scary part. When people think we are "religious" and we start to believe them. When people praise us to be a certain way and we suddenly think they're right.

So to all the hijabis and thobe-ies and huffadh and khatib and anyone doing any Islamic Dawah and giving naseeha. Be wary. Be careful. Constantly renew intentions. Make sure that secret prayer you pray in the cloves of night is far greater than the ones you pray in public. Make sure that you aren't attending the events for the wrong reasons. Make sure you aren't organizing events for the wrong reasons. Make sure that when people praise you - you reject their praise and seek refuge with Allah. For He hid your flaws and sins and He can easily show the truth.

And because you don't want all of this hard work to disappear and the doors of Jannah to close in front of you because of "one atom of Pride".

—— —— ——

"Guilt is a gift from Allah warning you that what you are doing is violating your soul."

The guilt can go away, if you don't succumb to it, and you continue to feel guilty, eventually, you'll become immune to the guilt.

That's how shaytaan makes it seem like half the things we do are totally okay and not violating our soul.

So the first time you saw something inappropriate on tv, it felt wrong, you hid it from your mom, you changed the channel, you closed your eyes. But now, bikinis don't phase you, kissing doesn't bother you, I mean, full on nudity doesn't stop you from watching Game of Thrones right? Shamelessness on TV, how normal Shaytaan has made it for us that we can continue to watch these things even during the month of Ramadan.

The first time you learned cursing, it was bad. But now, they come out like liquid, gushing from your lips at any moment of anger or frustration. For some, even moments where there is no reason at all to curse.

And the holy grail problem for majority of the Muslim youth today: Free-mixing. Because really, I mean, you're not committing zina, so what harm could come from a co-ed iftaar together. The boys won't sit next to the girls, they'll be across them. No one is going to hold hands or anything. There is a difference between professional meeting for work related purposes. And leisure. And you know the difference, you don't need someone to spell it out for you. Can you just imagine the angels recording the event, sad, drooping, angels that would much rather spend the month listening to you recite Quran than be there?

Before, that guilt existed. But for many of us, it has faded.

We need to get it back because that guilt is our compass of what is right and what is wrong. That guilt is the blessing from Allah that says our hearts haven't hardened, our hearts aren't black. The guilt is the purpose behind why He created us - to worship, to repent.

— — —

"Never forget - every time you get addicted to your body, whether it's constantly looking in the mirror or traveling two boroughs for a dessert. Remember that you are not a body; you are a spirit. Think to yourself, I wonder what I really look like - when this mask comes off." - Ustaadh Mohammad Elshinawy

At the end of the day, it is basically a persona. Under the niqaab, abaya, hijab, thobe, beard - behind the "niceness" and "religiousness" and all the perceptions people have of you - you are someone to Allah.

Now people can have bad perceptions. That you're a fake and you've committed despicable sins, to be honest, I've heard people accuse girls of zina without a second thought. But even behind those personas - you are someone to Allah.

It's your decision - it's up to you who you want to be to Allah.

No one else knows if you're actually concentrating in your prayer. No one else knows if you're attending a lecture for the knowledge or to catch a glimpse of a certain someone, or to give off the vibe that you're "religious". No one else knows if you're actually praying sunnah because you do so all the time or because everyone is seeing you so you want to look extra good. No one else knows if you're awake at night on facebook or watching inappropriate things, or if you're praying Qiyaam. No one else knows if you're carrying the mushaf out of habit and because you actually read it - or to give the look of "religiousness" and to post pics on snapchat.

Even if people know you do such-and-such - no one knows you like Allah.

So stand in front of a mirror and metaphorically strip off the facade - how clean is your soul.

Are there ink spots of jealousy, of envy, of lust, of greed. Is there charcoal from repetitive sins you just can't let go of. Is there tar stuck from things you haven't truly repented for.

Are you only an apparition of light for others - but carry none of it inside yourself. Are people in love with your perceived piety but the angels can't stand the smell of you.

People are searching their whole lives for the truth, and you have it laying on your desk or tucked in a cabinet. Iqraa.

— — —

"None of us will do work that is equivalent to the reward of Jannah"
-- Ammar AlShukry

This is really a paraphrase of a hadith that says the only way we are getting into Jannah is through the mercy of Allah, not our own efforts.

But I want to flip the story a bit.

"I'm going to hell anyway"

With that attitude, yeah, you probably are, since shaytaan has convinced you SO much that your miniscule tower of bad deeds is SO terrible that Allah can't forgive you.

That entire phrase is blasphemous. That PROVES you don't know the first thing about "Bismillahi Ar Rahman Ar Raheem" the two names of Allah that you mention many times on any given day.

For you to think that you not wearing hijab or not praying enough or maybe even drinking or having a haraam relationship - that these things can OUTWEIGH the mercy of Allah - I mean really, how arrogant can you be?

So Allah can forgive people who have denied His existence and then finally turned around and proclaimed His oneness - but oh no, you are so terrible that the Lord of the Universe, the Master of every being on this planet, past, present, and future - that Lord can't possibly forgive a tiny, insignificant human being like you for your tiny mountain of sins.

OKAY. Congrats on making Shaytaan smile, and please, give Allah the credit He deserves, and come back. It's time to come back. Your Lord is waiting.

— — —

"Allah gave us our organs, our health and our beauty but we take those blessings and use them to sin against Allah. You gave me my eyes, but I'm still going to watch haraam. You gave me my beauty but I won't wear hijab. I will use my blessings against you. But the epitome of His generosity is that He still continues to give you your blessings." - Dr. Farhan Abdul Azeez

The scary reality of this statement. Because whenever we sin - we use a facet that we barely even thank Allah for. How many of us lay in bed at night and say "thank you Allah for my eyesight and my hearing and my capable feet and hands and fingertips and tongue", do we even thank Him for the bed we sleep on?

Every single one of us sins. But we need to catch that we have sinned and automatically repent.

And we need to stop belittling our sins. It's not about if it's a minor sin or a major sin - it's about the greatness and majesty of the Lord you are sinning against.

So watching the movie isn't a little haraam. If you're not committing a sin but the actors are - are you in the clear?

So being just friends isn't a little haraam. So listening to cursing in rap songs isn't a little haraam. So forgetting to pray isn't a little haraam.

If you truly believed in Allah, you'd know of His majesty and His wrath. And you'd be hopeful in His mercy but fearful of His wrath.

Find a sin you do. And vow to stop. This moment. This instant. You'll fail perhaps. You may do it again. But promise yourself to stop. And that's your promise. In a quiet room, between you and Allah, you promise to stop this particular sin.

Don't overthink. Just do it. You aren't an angel, you have a sin. What sin do you want to wipe off permanently. Who do you want to be?

Slave of Allah. Resident of Jannah. Pay your dues and pay your fines and don't delay your own reward.

———

"Shaytaan beautified the very thing that lead our mother and father to be banished from Paradise. And that was the removal of the clothes. As the first gift of paradise is the clothes of paradise, Shaytaan wanted Adam and Eve to be humiliated and what's more humiliating that to be exposed in public."

But now. Well. That's the norm. We don't even flinch at the sight of a bikini. We don't even feel fazed at men's thighs. Billboard and ads. Movies and tv shows. Navels deemed okay by the cultural attire in Bollywood films. Bare breasts can go on the big screen, rated M, but you can still watch it in a room full of people without embarrassment. Netflix barely has filters, Wolf on Wall Street was supposed to be classy. Fifty Shades of Grey is part of pop culture. And everything is twerking.

Did you need a reality check to show you the indecency that has infiltrated your life? Or are you of those who possess haya, enough to lower your gaze when a mere second of haram comes up.

Cause yes you may have become immune. Yes you can blame society. Yes you can blame shaytaan. But shaytaan may have blown dust over society, are you willing to let him influence you too? Isn't it scary how you could sacrifice your entire akhira because you think you can simply blame shaytaan? Sacrificing eternal paradise for a few hours of entertainment?

You can fight the immunity - you can get it back. You can sensitize yourself again. Go a month without TV and movies and music videos - I promise it is doable. I swear by Allah that life is possible without these things. That your body and your eyes will become uncomfortable by certain things if you just start lowering your gaze.

And that is the mark of a believer - hayaa is a mark of a Muslim.

— — —

"You have to make sure the cup is clean before you pour in the clean water." - Sheikh Samer Alraey

It's really difficult to all of a sudden start doing a million good deeds or even acquire a lot of knowledge if you are still holding onto so many sins.

You will sin. It is natural. But reflect on your life - weren't there time periods where you didn't sin as much as you do now? Or vice versa - where you visually remember that you sinned so much more than you do now?

Acquire knowledge, become a student of knowledge, but let go of the sins because they're holding you back.

There are the big obvious ones that glare at you - the ones who hide from the world (like pornography addiction or smoking), the ones you hide from religious people in your community (relationships or friends the opposite gender), the ones you feel uncomfortable even to process (like the insurmountable ribaa on your loans). The big ones are obvious to even yourself because when you [cut off] gathering, there is a feeling in your gut, a sense inside y[cut off] are a sinner.

The "small" ones are harder to grasp, perhaps harder to fix. (Small in quotes because Allah is great and no sin is really small if it's against the Almighty). But these sins - they're normalized. The talking back to parents, the cursing, the inappropriate shows, the gossip that doesn't feel like gossip, the cheating on exams.

For everyone who is trying to become "religious" or "practicing" - let go of a sin first. Find one, any one, and let go of it.

Or else you're really just going to lecture after lecture and accumulating stuff. But you're judged on your actions, not your knowledge.

You can't continuously sin and think that a few nawafil will make it up and then go back to that same sin. Reading Quran every day is not going to stop you from sinning unless you physically stop yourself.

Imaan is not a magical button.

Stop pouring the water in your cup if it's still muddy inside.

Filter your heart, take away the judgement, envy, jealousy, materialistic need. Make space for purity.

The Quran won't enter a blackened heart.

Why would Allah give you a gift if you wouldn't use it correctly or cherish it properly?

— — —

We know that we don't get into Jannah by virtue of our good deeds; we really get in because of Allah's mercy. But with that aside, there are eight gates to jannah.

We could potentially aim at one of those gates, if not multiple. The one for prayer, the one for fasting, the one for controlling one's anger, the one for constant dhikr.

You have no idea which deed Allah will accept - He only needs to t would be enough to grant you into Jannah.

Ramadan nights is what He accepts, or maybe
ly small, like the glass of water you got your
f chocolate you got your friend, or that one time
noon and said SubhanAllah, or that one train ride
d to Quran.

You mi.. .inking, alright, I'm covered then. I pray, I do my dhikr
sometimes, and I'm super nice to my friends.

But what about the other deeds. The ones you push to the back of
your head because the guilt of it eats at you.

What about the time you leaked someone's secret, broke someone's
trust, backbit, cursed, sins of the tongue so normalized and abundant.

What about sins of the eyes: it's the modern age, sexual objectification
sold as freedom by a society that still can't create enough films to pass
the Bechdel test.

Sins of the eyes in secret, at 1AM when all you hear is the minifan
inside your laptop; sins of the eyes in open, scenes of women gyrating
their pelvis in unison with barely any clothes, normalized because it's
part of "culture" be it eastern or western. Imagine you died exactly
at that moment, with that scene on the screen - that's the moment
the angels came. Will they be saying salaam to you or will they be
yanking your heart out, disgusted.

And sins of the ears that only lead your heart to get colder and colder
so the Quran doesn't seem to "work", it doesn't make you melt, it
doesn't make you cry.

So you have a lot of good deeds, perhaps more than the bad deeds.

And the bad deeds - well if everyone's doing it, it can't be that bad,
right?

That's your call. Do you want to risk your Jannah for it?

— — —

Story: There's a fisherman who throws in the juiciest looking worm as bait and waits. A young fish is about to head to the worm when an older fish stops the young fish and says "Don't go there. If you eat the worm, it'll taste good for a little bit, but then you'll get hooked. And then you'll go above the water and meet these creatures called humans. And the humans will gauge out your eyes and use a knife to cut you into pieces and barbeque you. And then they will eat you and it'll digest in their stomachs and you don't want to know what happens next." So the young fish swims around the worm to see if he can see the humans or the knives they'll use to cut him. He saw none of it. So he ate the worm and although it was juicy at first, he got hooked.

"So many scholars say to stay away from something seemingly insignificant because you'll get hooked." - Sheikh Muntasir Zaman

The problem is that once you're hooked - it just goes downhill from there.

Like the ayah about the forbidden fruit in Jannah - the sin was eating the fruit. But the ayah says Allah told Adam AS "Do not go near this tree." (2:35) The command was to stay away from the tree.

So there are all these seemingly small insignificant things that aren't technically haraam ... yet. Like groups of friends who might not be the best of influences and it's not haraam to be hanging out with them - but if they're swearing in every other sentence, womanizing/ lusting men, trash talking others, drinking, smoking, blasting profane music - well then you are touching haraam even if you yourself aren't swallowing it.

And you already know what "don't go near the tree" covers. Trust yourself, there's that little tiny voice or that little twist in your tummy right before you go near the tree that says "errr, is this okayy..." and then a part of your nafs says "mehhh, is it really a big deal? like come on. Everyone does this stuff. This is normal. This is the modern day. Get with the program. It's not even a huge sin, is it even a sin? I know myself. I would never do the real sin."

And when you override that tiny voice and continuously override it, time after time, it gets quiet. You get hooked. And it's not until you

25

get into some deep trouble that you'll realize that you need to end it.

For a lot of people - it's not until they've had the weed rolled between their index finger and thumb, or until all the clothes have come off, or swears get slurred at their own mother - it's not until they're about to swallow or have already swallowed the sin - do they realize how close they've come to the tree, or high they have climbed upon it.

For others, through Allah's mercy and kindness - it doesn't go that far. They leave the circles, they leave the relationships, they stop the almost-xrated videos, they take a step back as soon as they are a foot away from the tree.

But the saabiqoon, the real winners, the ones who get that A+ level in Jannah - they can't even look at the tree out of disgust for the sin. They don't go near it out of fear of Allah but also out of love of Allah.

And may we all be amongst the saabiqoon. Ameen.

— — —

"Nobody is safe from the tongues of people. Even if he were to be the Prophet so pure. If one is silent, they say he is voiceless. And if he speaks, they say he talks much. Were he to fast and stand to pray at night. They say he's blind, he shows off, he deceives" - Imam al-Shafi'i

People will always have something to say. Don't listen to them.

Even the most well respected and knowledgeable of the people have someone out there saying 'He's a contradiction'. As much as you try, as much as you improve in deen, people will always talk about you. If it's not about your clothes, it's about your deeds, it's about your social life, your facebook status, or your opinions.

How many times have you been called a 'hypocrite'?

Everyone is human, everyone sins. Don't justify the sin - accept that what you did/do/are doing is haram, it's sinful. And change yourself - or try to. And people might not see you change, but keep the intention to change and try. It's your personal relationship with Allah, He's the one testing you - don't show the world your answers.

26

People will always find your flaws and try to show them off to the world. People will always have something to say.

That's why our goal is to please Allah. Not people.

— — —

"You don't hide sins you've repented for from people to be dishonest. If you've made tawba, the sin is removed completely. So why talk about something that hasn't happened?"

Oh, this is so important.

Because we do it so often in terms of other people's sins. We have all done this. We have all held on to an image of someone based upon what they did in the past.

And a whole year or five can go by and we will still think that person used to smoke, that girl was always at hookah bars, that boy was always high, that girl took off her hijab, they had a girlfriend/boyfriend, they ate haraam, they partied, they lied. We hold judgements of people from their past sins.

But change can happen. And change does happen. If our entire body changes completely every 7 years, how can our spirituality and our intellect ever remain a constant? If you have changed and matured and learned and fell and stood up again within the past few years - why aren't other people capable of the same thing?

Would you love who you were a year back? Two years back? Five years back? Yet we can judge someone we knew back in high school, back in college. Even if we aren't outwardly backbiting about their past sins (which is scary because one, we shouldn't backbite, two, we are talking about something that was already forgiven which puts us in a terrible place in the eyes of Allah because it is as if we are competing with Allah and His right to judge), we are still judging inwardly and holding onto a facade.

The greatest of scholars, the greatest caliphs, the people in the highest levels of Jannah - every single one has sinned. Some sinned repeatedly, sins that are unimaginable. But every sinner gets a chance to enter the garden, and we are not to judge them on that, we are not to hinder them on changing.

So be wary. Because change is possible. Give people the benefit of doubt, give people mercy, close your eyes, focus on yourself.

"Some people have the disease of criticising all the time. They forget the good about others and only mention their faults. They are like flies that avoid the good and pure places and land on the bad and wounds. This is because of the evil within the self and the spoiled nature." Ibn Taymiyyah

— — —

"Whoever gives up something for the sake of Allah, Allah will compensate him with something better than it." (So most people attribute this to the Prophet SAW saying it's classed saheeh by Al-Baani, but I didn't find an accurate source - Allahu A'lam)

But we do believe that when we give up something for Allah, He does reward us. Especially if it's something we want, or our body wants.

For example, we give up sleep to wake up on time for fajr, or to pray thahajjud, or qiyaam or read Quran at night. We give up food and drink in order to fast extra fasts. We are giving up things our body needs or wants - out of wanting to please Allah.

At first, it's hard, it's painful. The same goes for other things we choose to give up - like giving up being involved in a lot of cultural things like dance performances, like giving up smoking, like giving up a haraam show you might like - be it Game of Thrones or Grey's Anatomy, or giving up Bollywood movies and that Bollywood music culture, or giving up showing your hair in order to observe hijab.

Like giving up talking to the person you love. Because you know it would displease Allah to continue. Because you know Allah doesn't bless the haraam. Because you want His pleasure more.

It's hard to give up things you like, but when you do it for His sake and His sake alone, He fills your heart with something better.

And when you find yourself missing your past habits, your past circles, the nights of binge watching shows - remind yourself of the contentment you found in giving it up. The contentment you found in qiyaam and Quran. Remind yourself that Allah is pleased with you giving it up. Remind yourself that Jannah has it all - and more.

"But you prefer the worldly life, even though the life hereafter will be better and will last forever." - Surah A'la

So don't prefer this life over the other. Pick something, and give it up, and do it for the sake of Allah.

— — —

"On the Day of Judgement you will not see any other book but your own book of deeds." - Sh. Omar Suleiman | Hard Earned: Tafseer of Surah Al-Qalam

This has something profound about it. On that day we will not be concerned about anyone else's book of deeds except our own. And in that same manner, we shouldn't be concerned with other people's book of deeds in this world.

This is not to say that when your friends are doing something stupid - you don't call them out on it. They're your friends for a reason - get them into Jannah with you so you can have the awesomest Jannah party ever. So remind them of praying, pull them into going to halaqas, share things with them. Call them out when they curse, call them out if they're about to do something haraam, sit them down and talk to them if they're in a haraam relationship. Save them. You're friends for the akhira, not just for the dunya. And let them save you. Let them fix your manners, your demeanour, your tajweed, your bad habits. When you slip up, let them catch you.

But don't bother yourself with other people's deeds. Good or bad. All you can do is make dua for them. But don't busy yourself with that.

Be concerned about your book. How many empty pages are left to fill? How many of them are charcoal black from the angels scribbling down your bad deeds, repeated ones, redundant ones, sighing as they have to write it again.

Etched into the pages are sins you forgot to seek forgiveness for: that time you missed fajr, the time you said something rude to your mother, the time you cursed out your sibling, the time you went to hookah bar, the time you prayed late because you were in the middle of a homework.

And in smudged ink, the sins you didn't think were really sins, like

29

the time you lied to a professor, or lied to a friend because you were ditching them, or lied to your parents about where you were, or the ribaa you have piling on your credit card bill and student loans, or when you broke a promise you made to a friend.

And how many pages are filled with light, liquid gold ink, the extra fasts you kept, the sadaqa you gave on the train ride to school, the way you consoled a friend. Rows and rows of tally marks for the number of rakats of qiyaam you did. Calligraphic writing listing the gifts you bought your mother and the verses of Quran you memorized.

And how many of the deeds might disappear, the beautiful ink vanishes and makes the page empty - because you had to give up those deeds to someone you hurt, to someone you slandered.

It's actually kind of insane, how easily we can trash talk celebrities and their personal lives. Wouldn't it be tragic - if on the day of judgement, Allah takes away those things you once had beautifully scripted into your book, and gives it to someone you didn't even know.

— — —

"Anger is the feeling - yelling is your choice." - Sh. Yaser Birjas

It's not the feeling that gets you the sin - but it's the action the feeling might evoke.

There's a really interesting nuisance from Surah Al-Isra that says not to say "uff" to parents. See, Allah doesn't say "do not get angry" at your parents. He says not to say "uff" - which is like modern day - ughhh, whateverrrrr, ohmygodddd, *rolls eyes*. It is not that you won't get angry - it is natural to get angry. But it is to not SHOW that you are angry at them because you are to remember the mercy they had upon you as they were raising you.

When you feel down - you decide whether to get yourself up and pray and read Quran and go be social, or pump up the music and smoke.

Liking, lusting, craving - all of these are feelings you are allowed to have, it is Allah that gave it to you in the first place - it's a blessing to have it - it means you're alive, and all the hormones are working.

But it's your choice - what do you choose to do about it. You choose to go to the Rated X websites with your doors locked, you choose to read inappropriate literature, you choose to go out to dinner, to go to a hotel, to go to the movies. Or you choose to fast, to suppress, to approach parents, to exert energy elsewhere, to work out. Ultimately, it's the action that translates into the deed - good or bad. It's the action that's being written down by the angels.

So whatever feeling it may be - if it elicits a reaction that would be harmful to someone else or harmful to your own imaan - don't do it. Understand the feeling, calm it down, find appropriate channels - be it through writing or by talking to someone extremely close to you.

& always remember, the ayah from Surah Az-Zumar - "O My servants who have transgressed against themselves [by sinning], do not despair of the mercy of Allah. Indeed, Allah forgives all sins."

— — —

"Don't give up hope in Allah and destroy your dunya and your akhira." - from Sheikh Omar Suleiman Tafseer of Surah Maryam.

You don't pray. Fine. Bow down now. It doesn't matter what prayer, just pray something, anything. You did drugs. Fine. Throw it out now. Flush it down. Doesn't matter how much the stash cost you because it is costing you so much more in the long run. You're in a haraam relationship. Just stop. Cold turkey. None of that waning off period where you're still friends because "trees of paradise aren't made from the seeds of hell".

You think Allah can't forgive?

If you truly believed in Allah - you'd know that your sins do not compare to His mercy. And you wouldn't doubt yourself. (and you'd also know that His wrath is real, and you wouldn't keep overstepping).

All the "religious" people you know didn't magically become practicing. Allah had to push them to their knees too.

So what exactly are you waiting for. Ring. Ring. This is your wake up call.

— — —

31

"If Allah takes you in - you are protected. If you're outside of this fold, the shaytaan devours you. Only you are at fault if you let shaytaan in your life." - Ustaadh Mohammad Elshinawy

You know when you first discovered Islam. Like really discovered it - not Sunday school force fed. Like when you first fell in love with this religion. You were on this cloud nine, you finally understood, your heart swelled up, and it all made sense.

And then you fell off this high. Maybe you got in the wrong crowd. Maybe you didn't have a support system. Maybe no one around you cared about Islam the way you did. Or maybe you just had a lot of hardships and couldn't pass the tests that were given to you by Allah. So you stepped outside the fold of Allah's protection.

You no longer cared for the extra good deeds - you were fine with being mediocre, just getting by, you're a Muslim right, so why do you have to be a good Muslim? Why do others get to party and do haraam and still no affliction seems to come their way?

When you step outside - shaytaan becomes your best friend. His goal is to bring you down to Hell with him. And it's so easy to do that when you're alone. When you're not busy with Quran or busy with your prayers or busy with your halaqas. It's so easy to make you sad, make you disheartened, make you want to "feel" something and guide you towards sex/porn, drugs, partying, smoking.

But when you're busy - with the worship of Allah, it's impossible for him to penetrate through. Because every action that you do glorifies Allah.

You see things and immediately seek refuge from Him, you see something beautiful and immediately praise Him, you feel some discomfort and immediately ask Him for relief, you get overwhelmed by work/papers/exams and immediately ask for ease.

How can shaytaan get to you when you're so busy loving Allah and bowing to Him?

"Shaytaan can only appeal to those for whom Allah is not enough."

— — —

Hassan Al-Basri was asked: "Shouldn't one of us feel too shy to ask his Lord to forgive his sin, then do it again, then ask for forgiveness, then do it again?" He said: "The Shaytaan wishes that you would have this attitude, so do not tire of asking for forgiveness". [Al-Jaami Al-Ulum]

Sincere repentance means that we promise to Allah not to commit the sin again. Let's say a sin like cheating on exams. We do it, and ask for forgiveness, and somehow we do it again. And we ask for forgiveness. But then it feels like, am I even being forgiven, since I keep doing it over and over again, what's the point in seeking for the forgiveness. -- that, is shaytaan talking because he wants control over you, he doesn't want you to go to Allah with your pile of sins, he wants you to stay a sinner, never get it wiped clean, and every time you do get it wiped clean, he wants to make a new pile for you, and then for you to be so overwhelmed by your sins that you give up.

This is not to say that you should sin, and say "oh if I do the sin again, I'll just ask for forgiveness and Allah will forgive me" - NO, you think you can fool Allah? When He's the one who knows everything. He knows exactly the way you think and how you are and your REAL intentions.

This is to say that do not despair in the greatness of your Lord. Do not despair in His mercy and His forgiveness.

If you've never prayed before, start today.

Allah's mercy is not limited. You're the one that hasn't asked for it enough.

— — —

"Islam is a religion of little victories. It asks you, are you better than you were yesterday." - Ustadh AbdelRahman Murphy

Every single day is a new opportunity for you to become the person you want to be in the future. Scratch that - every single hour, after every single prayer.

People think they need to wait for Hajj or something to become "sin-less" like a new born baby. But what has blinded you so much to not believe that God has already forgiven all your sins and does so whenever you ask Him to.

Prayer is a way to wash off your sins. So, technically, if Allah answers your cry for forgiveness - you're a new born baby after every single prayer. Take advantage of that! You are beautiful! You are blessed. You are pure.

Feel Him cleaning out the specks of darkness in your heart and then change. Become that religious person you want to become. Become the one who prays more than what is asked for. Become the role model you want to be for your future children. Become the person you always wished you could be.

Because, "heaven is filled with sinners who repented".

— — —

"When we go to the Prophets that day to ask them to intercede on our behalf, they will all keep saying "nafsi" (myself). If the prophets at that time are going to say this. Imagine us." - Dr. Farhan Abdul Azeez

So imagine how selfish we would be at that moment. When we are drenched in sweat. Running around everywhere, knowing that we can't bow and get any more deeds.

Knowing that it's too late. If only we prayed one more rakat. If only we prayed on time. If only we were sincere in our prayers.

And when Prophets who were selflessly struggling hardship after hardship, when they say 'Oh Allah, save me.' Who are we? These people devoted their life to Allah and we just pray for ten minutes a day and call that devotion. Some of us just believe in Allah and think that's sufficient.

They are scared of the wrath of Allah and we just pat ourselves in the back for being decent human beings, not cursing, and praying five times.

Ibraheem AS was willing to sacrifice his own beloved son just because God commanded Him to do so but we can't even wear hijab properly or lower our gaze or give up certain forms of entertainment.

And we want the Jannah that they're going to be granted?

We want the same Jannah that children in Syria and Palestine and Africa and Burma and Bangladesh and Pakistan etc - the orphans walking around begging for food, the oppressed seeing their relatives murdered in front of them, the silenced women constantly raped, the innocent in Guantanamo, the abused children, the Jannah that they are going to get - we want THAT Jannah? The SAME Jannah as them?

What did you do today to even deserve something as beautiful and as permanent as Jannah?

———

"True imaan is when you're no longer tempted by disobedience and corruption. True imaan is when you are disgusted by these things." - Ustaadh Nouman Ali Khan

It's one thing to become more practicing and still half kind of want to go back. Like longing for those mixed gatherings and parties where gender boundaries are obsolete. Like wanting to go back to smoking and chilling day in and day out. Or wanting to go back to watching pornography. Or somehow trying to justify the severity of the sin and minimize it so that you could potentially go back.

You haven't reached the pinnacle of your own imaan if you still crave and want certain haram things. Haram is supposed to be revolting. Shaytaan beautifies it - so for majority of us, some haram does seem to reel us in. But we have to actually build that imaan.

And the imaan will not come until you have a few things down - like praying all five prayer on time & praying sunnahs & reading Quran every day.

At the end of the day, all you have in the grave is you. Your mom and best friend and spouse will not be there for you.

So it's up to you how you wish to be. A person with unfaltering imaan or a person with weak imaan.

Do you want to be questioned about every little thing you did or do you want that free pass with the Prophet SAW, straight to Jannah, no questions asked.

Because I can't imagine standing in front of Allah, muttering half justifications for the long list of sins, and begging, sujood after sujood to hide them and just erase them.

— — —

These are Mahatma Gandhi's Seven Deadly Sins, and I'm going attempt to take you through each one of them using an Islamic lens:

Wealth without work: The concept of haram money - one of the many reasons why gambling is a sin - it takes luck, not hardwork, to make the money. It's also another reason that Ribaa - lending money on interest is haram.

Pleasure without conscience: Allah did not say not to have pleasure in this world - but to be conscience about the rulings He laid for us. Sex isn't haram. As a matter of fact sex after marriage gets rewarded - you get rewarded for pleasing your spouse through physical activity. But complete and utter pleasure where you intoxicate yourself and lose conscience - is wrong.

Science without humanity: Maybe this is complicated to explain but science can't explain if there is a God or not - science can't explain miracles or supernatural things. Can science explain love? And on a more practical understanding: using animals for the purpose of scientific advancement still requires compassion and understanding limitations. For example, using animals for cosmetic sciences is a tad inhumane.

Knowledge without character: Knowledge is useless if you don't put it into action. Like people who memorize the Quran and spew hadiths but go home to beat their wife and kids.

Politics without principle: I think this is self explanatory. The purpose of the political system is to protect the community and the voices of the people, not to make money and steal oil.

Commerce without morality: Business without morals - using child labor, or go even beyond that to just the business of prostitution or go to the pornography industry.

Worship without sacrifice: Don't think you're going to be a pious person without sacrifice. You have to sacrifice certain pleasures of this world - like the drinking and partying. You have to sacrifice time to pray and read Quran.

— — —

Sins leading to Jannah

"Verily, a slave commits a sin and thereby enters Jannah [because of it] and he preforms a good deed and enters Hell because of it."
- Imaam Ibn al-Qayyim (from the book Al-Waabil As-Sayyib Min Kalaam At-Tayyib)

How so?

"[This is because] he commits the sin and he does not cease shedding tears concerning it, fearing [its consequence] regretting it, feeling shameful before his Lord the Most High. Hanging his head low with a broken heart, because of this, the sin is in truth more beneficial for him as it is the source of many good deeds after it. And through it the slave attains salvation and success, so much so that this sin becomes the reason for the slave to enter jannah [i.e through the mercy of Allah].

And he [might] preform a good deed and does not cease in mentioning that, and feeling full of pride and is amazed at himself saying "I did and I did!" [i.e boasting] so pride enters [his heart] which results in his destruction."

A sin can lead you closer to Allah. Do not despair. Do not despair.

— — —

"I'm a human being. I make mistakes. I'm flawed"

I think we forget this when it comes to our fellow brothers and sisters. Well, number one we shouldn't be judging at all because Allah is the one and only judge since He knows what is truly in people's hearts. But sometimes we make assumptions about people and even idealize situations.

Say a sister once partied and drank and did inappropriate things in public and dated. And then let's say she became more religious and started observing hijab and what not. Who are we to say "She's just faking". And then let's say a few years later she even took off the hijab. Who are we to say "Astaghfirullah she's turning so bad". Allah gives everyone different tests. Maybe she's having difficulty passing hers. Maybe she'll pass hers with great marks because 10 years down the line - you may be the one wearing skinny jeans and hijab while she is holding a Quran with her full abaya.

And on this point - another thing we may sometimes forget is that scholars are human beings too. Our teachers, our speakers, they can stumble upon their words here and there. Don't commit shirk and put them up on a pedestal. Admire their knowledge and their ability to practice it to such a great level but see them as merely human - with their own sins and own flaws.

Everyone gets tested in different ways.
Everyone sins differently.
We must simply focus on ourselves.

"Blessed is the person who is so busy fixing his or her own faults, that they don't have time to look at the faults of others." — Br. Wisam Sharieff

———

Reflections from Story Night: Accused with Ustaadh Nouman Ali Khan.

The entire lecture made me reflect on two sides: one of the victim and one of the perpetrator - because each of us have been on both ends.

By victim I mean - you have heard people talk about you. Be it rumors or whispers in the hall, be it on formspring, on myspace pages, on xanga, on facebook pages, on tumblr - and the world of the anonymous questioners. You've heard whatever was said about you or you've seen the screenshots. Sometimes it's "small" things, like the girl who took off her hijab for a party, or rumors about a guy and weed. Sometimes it's actual accusations on your chastity, on your purity, on your "religiosity".

By perpetrator I mean - you have said something. You have mentioned a secret maybe you didn't know was a secret. You affirmed a rumor with no basis. You asked a question that implied something. You shared a picture or screenshot you shouldn't have.

You were "seeking advice about whether to approach someone about something."

So look at the following things from both ends - the times when you were hurt by words that came back to you and the times when you said something you shouldn't have.

"Those who throw something, even suggesting something, at dignified women - that is enough to get 80 lashes as punishment in THIS dunya."

[Now now, this doesn't mean men who suggest things about their fellow sisters - this includes girls. Girls who suggest someone might be in a relationship, girls who suggest that someone was seen holding hands with someone, girls who suggest that someone had a "past".]

"You started a chain reaction and you will have a share of that sins. This means whoever you shared something to - you get the sins of whomever that person decides to share that something too. So night and day, there are sins being counted against you. PEOPLE ARE SINNING ON YOUR BEHALF."

[If that is not horrifying - I don't know what is. Imagine you BARELY said something, like I heard so-and-so posted such on instagram - and then someone takes that and spreads that to a few other people who add things to it and it just keeps going. And you - oblivious to what you did, you praying your qiyaam and fasting your fasts - gathering all the good deeds you can, only to find your hands empty on the day of judgement as the sins other people accumulated on your behalf overburden you.]

"When you speak about another Muslim, you're hurting your own self - we are one ummah, we are one body."

"The principle is - when a fellow Muslim is being accused, your first response is "this is a lie". [even if] you don't know the facts - but you know the Quran! And the Quran says to say this."

"In a setting when this is happening your response should not be to stay quiet. It should be to say "this is none of our business" and then to say "subhan-aka". Not SubhanAllah. Subhan-aka is you speaking

39

directly to Allah. To bring awareness to yourself and everyone present that there is another witness to this conversation and that is Allah."

"Your intentions may be good - that doesn't make it right."

[This is the thing. This is the core. Ustaadh Nouman was explaining how most of us talk out of concern for others. We are not evil people who enjoy talking ill of others or making up rumors and spreading them. We talk because we care about them. But that still doesn't make it right.]

The term 'fahisha' in the Quran, usually refers to indecency - usually illegal sexual intercourse, spreading shameless - but in this ayah it refers to the people who tarnish other people's reputation. (*SIDENOTE* If you only read English translation - you would MISS the ENTIRE point of this ayah 24:19. Because without tafseer, it is almost always translated as 'illegal intercourse' or 'spreading immorality' - it doesn't emphasize that this is referring to spreading conversation that zinna happened, not that actual zinna happened.)

"The ayah says that if we are guilty of tarnishing someone's reputation - painful punishment will come to us in this life and the hereafter."

[And many times the punishment is like karma - the same happens to you. You spoke like this about others and others spoke like this about you.]

"[In terms of the ayah about good women are for good men] - it doesn't mean they didn't have a past. It means they may have had a past but repented from it and now they have become good. [. . .] and for good people, there will always be people talking ill of them."

"In this world you [the person who brought forward the rumor] couldn't bring four witnesses to make your case - on the day of judgement I will bring forward five witnesses against you [the slander-er]: your tongue, your hands, and your limbs."

[Your tongue because you spoke of a person like that, your hands - Allah knew we would be texting these things - your limbs, everywhere you went to talk about this person.]

"Saving our own dignity by saving the dignity of others."

And Allah has saved the punishment for you - you who had a share in spreading something. And Allah tells the victims not to worry - He is the witness. He is the all wise.

In a way - it is comforting to know that it's okay if people talk crap, Allah knows of your true self, and you'll get their good deeds on the day you need it most, and Allah will punish them severely.

In a way - it's uncomfortable to realize how accountable you are, how easily the good deeds you have will slip through your fingers onto the scales of people - people who may have been your "friends" or may have been random people or maybe celebrities. How harshly you will be punished for words you thought were "light". For suggestions - not accusations. You didn't say anything at all but you insinuated it.

"It's no longer a matter between you and the people. IT IS NOW A MATTER OF YOUR RELATIONSHIP WITH ALLAH."

— — —

Sins feel good. Temporarily. Because shaytaan beautifies them. It feels good to take off hijab and let loose. It feels good to dance in front of a stage of a thousand people after practicing for months. It feels good to get light headed. It feels good to have someone the opposite gender comfort you. It feels good to watch porn.

It feels disgusting afterwards. You rebelled against your own soul. You disobeyed the Creator of the World. You disobeyed the very God that gave you your sight and your senses and your joints and your sustenance.

People who have committed these kinds of sins know how it tastes. They are constantly tempted to go back because it is so unbelievably easy to go back. On top of that - they also don't know if Allah accepted their repentance.

It could be years and years later - and the pushed memory of their sin drifts into their head as a voice whispers "And you still think you deserve Jannah? And you think you're good enough to touch the Quran? And you think you deserve a righteous spouse? And you want to be a religious person?"

Sins are haunting.

And for those who think - damn, everyone else gets to have so much fun or these newly-practicing Muslims had so much fun.

A speaker once said "Do you think Allah just wants us to suffer while everyone else is having fun? He prohibited things because it's in our best interest."

So take a moment to think about it. The things that displease Him - what if they were permissible?

It would affect the entire ummah as a whole. It would affect your very nature. Your character wouldn't be the way it is.

If things like drugs, swearing, clubbing etc - were allowed. Your ears would be immune to the filthiness because it wouldn't be considered filthy. Your days would be less productive, your happiness would be so dependent upon a substance, your money would be wasted on these intoxicants rather than charity. Lose interactions of the genders - well I think we all know what that leads to - forget children growing up without a family unit or knowing who their father is - but emotional suffering, heartbreak, going through break ups consistently, adultery widespread, it would be normal for your wife to be dancing against another man, as it would be normal for your husband to be staring at a woman's behind.

And I'm not saying these issues don't exist in the Muslim ummah regardless - they do.

But it is the wisdom of Allah that He tells us to stay away.

Don't even go near the sin. He knows what it leads to. Even the things we don't understand - even things we can't rationalize, because this is all just rationalizing. He holds His wisdom. We just need to accept that.

The best of nations. You are a part of the best of nations. You are to have the best of characters. You are to be the best people to walk on this earth - to the trees and the animals and the people.

Rewind: 1) You don't know that if you were put in the middle of the sinful life, would you have come out of it. 2) Those who lived a part of their life engrossed in sin have struggles and pains and a haunting that is unimaginable to others. 3) These sins that are romanticized and idealized and glorified and beautified, all have a price. And a reason behind why Allah made them sins is due to His wisdom.

And keep in mind that the people of Jannah are all sinners.

You just have to be the sinner that turns back. The sinner that runs to the good deeds. The sinner that always remembers the greatness of Allah, His majesty, and His mercy.

"O son of Adam, so long as you call upon Me and ask of Me, I shall forgive you for what you have done, and I shall not mind. O son of Adam, were your sins to reach the clouds of the sky and were you then to ask forgiveness of Me, I would forgive you. O son of Adam, were you to come to Me with sins nearly as great as the earth and were you then to face Me, ascribing no partner to Me, I would bring you forgiveness nearly as great as it." [Tirmidhi]

hardships
and
heartaches

"No need to complain of calamities, the illusion of a life lasts but a moment" - Sheikh Abu Saeed

If you think about bad moments in comparison to your life, it is so miniscule. Remember that time in elementary school when that horrible embarrassing thing happened? Or the friend you had in middle school that did something terrible to you? Or those horrifying finals and the SATs and those insane moments where you thought life couldn't get any worse? The financial problems, the family problems, the imaan problems, the friends problems and drama.

And then you were back on your feet again. Honestly, these terrible moments pass by. "Everyone wants happiness, no one wants pain. But you can't have a rainbow, without a little rain."

The bad moments make up barely a percentage of your life as a whole. Even if you have had bad months, you live about, say 80 years. So, do the math. Good moments, happy moments, content, peaceful moments. Those are far more.

And then - on an even greater level what is 80 years of life - to an eternity? This world is going to pass by. And then we have eternity. InshaAllah in Paradise. And oh the things we can do there - the people we get to meet and hang out with and talk to.

So don't fret it. Let the moments come and go. And when you go to bed at night, just think of Jannah. The eternal abode. And ask Allah for it before you sleep.

— — —

Often times when we see the highlight reel of other people's life - be it their snapchat, their instagram, their academic success, their wealth - we unintentionally feel like "They're so lucky." And sometimes that translates into "Why don't I have that."

But we don't see that with every blessing, they probably went through 100 hardships to get there.

I know of a couple, the night of their wedding, they spent on the floor of a basement - no furniture, no money, and student loans. They lived in that basement up until their second child. And now, they own a little mansion in the deep suburbs. And yet they give thousands every month to the masjid. The push money off and money seems to follow them. And it's literally the blessing of Allah (and simultaneously a test). But they passed their earlier test - that of having sabr during hard times.

When Allah gives a hardship, He already prepared the ease. You'll get the ease eventually. It'll come. It always has. It always does. It always will.

— — —

"The Beloved says, 'The broken ones are My darlings.' Crush your heart, be broken" -- Shaikh Abu Saeed Abil Kheir

Stop giving it away to the boy or girl, stop holding it out to the grades and the career. Steal all the pieces back and patch it together with dhikr and quran.

Chase after contentment and find it only in the worship of Allah.

Because the food, the tv shows, the video-games, the hookah, the booze, will only give you temporary relief. True relief from that type of pain can only come from the whispered sobs in sujood.

If Allah is the owner of hearts, where were you going anyway? What are you chasing?

All you need is the One that is closer to you than your jugular vein.

— — —

Reviewing the tafseer of Surah Jumuah by Ustaadh Nouman Ali Khan - and in the first ayah, we declare Allah's purity - which also means to declare that He is flawless.

And I realized - sometimes. We think we know what we should have gotten. We should have gotten this school, this internship, this job, this opportunity, this spouse.

And we think we know what's best for us. I mean, sure, we don't vocalize it. But inside - it's like, why, Allah? Why didn't you give me this? I worked so hard. I prayed so hard. How could you not give me this?

But that kind of questioning - means we think Allah is flawed.

It means we think He made a mistake.

Except Allah is Al-Malik, Al-Quddus, Al-Aziz, Al-Hakeem.

He is beyond our concept of space and time - He owns the universe, the seas, and your stubborn pumping heart.

His decisions, His timing, His rules.

Now it's just a matter of - do you trust Him? Do you firmly believe He's your Master? Isn't He Perfect?

— — —

"It's not that easy - you gotta make it through some things to get there." - Sheikh Omar Suleiman : Story of Jibreel

Don't you guys sometimes feel like it's the best people who go through the hardest struggle.

The woman who prays the longest, she's the one with the abusive husband. The women who covers the most has the disloyal husband.

The boy who recites the most beautifully and the most often, is the one struggling financially. The one with the best of manners, has rumors spurring about. The one who brings light to others, is the one who keeps dealing with family death. The one who prays the most prayers, getting accused of zina. The gentle and kind uncle is the one who gets the cancer while the greedy, malicious one is fine.

Sometimes if you really got to know the struggles of some people, it makes you almost question Allah - why them? Why do they fight the hardest battle? They don't deserve this.

Except they do - because this is their source of purification. They're the lucky ones that meet Allah purified. They're supposed to fight the hardest battle. They're supposed to get every curve ball. They're supposed to live a life full of hardship because they get to enter without questioning.

They spend their nights in prayer begging for Jannah. And this is how Allah gives them Jannah.

Jannah is surrounded with obstacles, trials, and tribulations.

But with hardship comes ease. And "notice it doesn't say 'after hardship comes ease' because the ease is already prepared."

The ease is the Jannah you seek after. So let the hardships come. Embrace them. They are your stepping stones to Jannah. Step with full faith, and have your sins wash away.

— — —

"Instead of cutting your body, let Allah mend your wounds."

There are lessons we wish we knew back then. When all we knew was of this immortal God we pray to five times a day. We knew nothing of His powers besides His wrath. We knew nothing of His healing.

You'd be surprised to find out the commonality of cutting. That your own beloved siblings or your own cherished cousins, as young as thirteen, may be covering their wrists.

And if you yourself can't comprehend why - try to. Understand that some people need their emotional pain to be manifested physically because physical pain is easier to handle, more tangible, they can see it.

And they need Al-Jabbar, but have no idea where to find Him. Maybe you're supposed to show them. But if you're behind your phone, too busy with your own friends, how will you take care of your flock, your family.

— — —

"This dunya is nothing but heartbreaks and heartaches; pack your suitcase and prepare for the akhirah. Keep it moving, this isn't your final destination."

You will never get what you want. Face that now. Accept it now. Because what you want is constantly changing, constantly evolving, constantly different. What you wanted as a child, what you wanted last year, what you want today, it's all different. And you've gotten things - you've gotten duas answered, pains taken away, materialistic gifts received, grades and peace and solutions.

But you will never get what you truly want in this world. All the money in the world - and still you won't get what you want.

Because what you want is to meet Allah. That's what you really want.

Jannah - that's just to explain that all your wishes will come true- your insane fantasies, the adornments, the luxury brand bags and watches, the wonderful cars, the gluttonous feasts, the wine and weed, the men and women of your pleasing, sunsets and sunrises and gardens and palaces.

Your final destination is more than that. It's sipping tea with your entire family, it's jumping on a full feather down bed with your best friend, it's sitting with the prophets, all of them, laughing your heart out at their jokes, it's seeing Aisha ra. hold Prophet Muhammad's (saw) hand. It's listening to your young grandparents tell you embarrassing stories of your mother. It's asking for rain and singing with Fatima RA, as it pours. It's talking to Adam AS, to Yusuf AS, to Ibraheem AS, asking him about building the Kaaba. It's seeing all the parents holding their crowns of light because their children were huffadh. It's seeing your parents actually show affection, with no signs of stress, no wrinkles, no worries. It's learning from your great-great grandchildren about how much technology changed when they were in the dunya.

It's sitting under His throne, asking Him all your confusing aqeedah questions, it's hearing Him welcome you with the word, salaam.

Do your part in this world, but don't plan on staying too long.

And whenever you're disheartened, whenever you are sad, remember the final destination, remember His mercy, and remember His promise.

"This life is a bridge, don't build upon it but cross over it."

— — —

"If you complain that Allah is testing you too much, you're failing the test." — Sheikh Omar Suleiman

Allah tests the ones He loves most. You think your life is hard? With all the luxuries of having a home, AC/Heat, clothing, water? Wait - forget starving orphans for a second. The prophets, each of them, what were their tests?

Did Allah ask you to take your spouse and newborn child to a random deserted place, leave them, never knowing whether they will survive or if you will ever see them again? Or to take your son and sacrifice him. Or to just be burned and have faith in Him. No, those were all Ibraheem (as)'s tests.

Did Allah ask you to put your newborn baby in a basket on the river and just trust Him? Or did you fight a bunch of wars and get stoned a bunch of times. Or slashed and whipped for proclaiming the belief of One God.

I'm not belittling your hardships, your sufferings. Because we all have our share of struggles. Deaths of family members, abuse, illnesses, financial conditions.

But remember that this isn't your world - the dunya is paradise for the disbelievers, but it's not OUR paradise - so Allah, give whatever hardships and tests you want, and help us pass them so we can go to Jannah.

— — —

"Success is like an iceberg ... most people will just see the surface but don't know what's beneath it."

When we see someone with success in their career we may say things like Allah has blessed them so much. Which is true. But the person also worked really hard to get there.

You don't know the number of nights they stayed awake, you don't know where they slept uncomfortably, you don't know about the times they chugged energy drinks to meet a deadline, you don't know the paper cuts, the headaches, the popping of painkillers.

When you see a hafidh, you're amazed that they have this book in their chest. But you don't know if they were forced through it at a young age, you don't know how they battled to balance their academic life with their Quran memorization life, you don't know how they struggle to retain it every single day, feeling scared they'll forget, scared they'll make mistakes, scared that they can't live up to the responsibilities in upholding the words of Allah.

When you walk into someone's beautiful home you feel like they're lucky, they must be rich, they must have no financial worries - but you don't know about the time when they lived in a small room and had one meal a day, wearing the same three items of cloth repetitively. You don't know the twenty-four hour shifts and juggling two or three jobs to save up enough for something as glamorous as they have now.

Success is a risq, it's all from Allah, but there are so many things that go into it too. The bottom of the iceberg - the hard work, the failures, the dedication, the good habits, the endurance, the sleepless nights, the sacrifices, the discipline, the criticism, the pillow wet with tears.

And you can have it too, maybe your iceberg is still growing in the bottom, the bottom is deeper than what shows on the surface. So the titles - hafidh, doctor, lawyer, teacher, engineer, 'alim, sheikh, writer, director, professor and more - they're titles that take deep icebergs.

"It's supposed to be hard. If it wasn't hard, everyone would do it. The hard is what makes it great."

— — —

"If there is one recipe for unhappiness it is that: expectations."
— Yasmin Mogahed

Guide to happiness, don't expect. Don't expect people to appreciate your work. Don't expect professors to be fair. Don't expect studying to always pay off. Don't expect from anyone.

Just know that Allah promised Jannah to the believers. And Allah never says "no" to a dua. So all you can do - truly - is do the best you can. Put in your all. And then ask Allah for whatever it is. And be content with the outcome. For He is the best of all Planners.

— — —

"Do not let your difficulties fill you with anxiety; after all it is only in the darkest nights that the stars shine more brilliantly." - Ali Ibn Al Thalib

Whenever you go through a struggle don't think it'll last forever, just pummel through it. There's always light at the end. And remember that every leaf on the earth moves by Allah's command so these struggles have reasons behind them. To test your patience, your strength, your endurance. And who did Allah give the hardest struggles to? The ones He loved most. So don't think "Ya Allah, why me? Why do I have to go through so much?" think of it like a blessing. Allah loves you THAT much.

— — —

"If your heart is broken, know that He is Al-Jabbar, the one who repairs."

And we know that any form of pain is a way for Allah to erase sins from our body. This means physical, mental and emotional pain.

So take heartbreak with stride. It's Allah calling you back.

It can be heartbreak from the loss of a loved one, from the distance of an old friendship, from the silence of someone you like.

Allah is with the broken hearted. So let Him fix it. And the easiest way to do that is to fall into sujood in the crevices of the night and sob. Sob like Allah's throne is in front of you and you are bowing down begging Him to fix your heart.

So forget the boy or girl who doesn't like you. Forget the friend who back stabbed you. Forget the people who left you. Forget the things people owe you.

In the end, you belong to Him and no one else. Why settle for anything less than an eternal life of pure happiness?

— — —

"The empire of the Pharoah and the oppression of the Pharoah, was destroyed by a baby in a basket." -- Ustaadh Nouman Ali Khan

This statement is referring to the concept of planning and Allah being the best planner. So when we get confused, when we think our story shouldn't end this way, remember that it's not the end.

Whatever is going on, from hardship to ease, there is more to this world, there is more to your biography. Trust that Allah has a beautiful story.

It's the same with the theory of a butterfly effect - small things impact life on a greater level. So the smallest things in your life are also part of Allah's master plan.

Now it's your call. Do you trust Him?

— — —

"Remember Me and I will remember you"

I was talking to a sister who was telling me how less than a three weeks ago, she was drinking and smoking weed. But now she has been praying all her prayers and waking up for fajr and reading Surah Yaseen, every - single - day.

How does that happen? How does someone who wasn't so close to the deen, flip switches and become that close. And if you saw this sister even now, you might not think she is that observant of her prayers or even picking up the Quran (this is being judgemental of her outer appearance, but that's a whole different story).

But how come some of us who are already on the path, can't seem to be as devoted as that? When was the last time we read the Quran after fajr?

Allah guides whom He wills but take a deep look at yourself. Are you at a stop sign? Can you no longer move ahead? Are your prayers perfunctory? Or are you tasting the honey of this commandment that God sent down?

And where are His words in the schema of your daily life?

— — —

"Mercy is not the emotion at the moment. Mercy is by the result of what happens. So if you hear a man is cutting off a guy's leg - you'll think - how is he merciful? Because you didn't realize that this man is a surgeon and the leg had a tumor. So it might be tough on you, but in the end, it is good for you." -- Sh. Samer Alraey

It's so easy to say. We reiterate it countless times, we give our friends the same advice, people give us this advice: Allah has better plans.

Allah knows what's good for you. Trust Allah. He loves you and he can only give you good.

The ayahs from the Quran share the same sentiment - "But perhaps you hate a thing and it is good for you; and perhaps you love a thing and it is bad for you. And Allah Knows, while you know not."

But when you're sitting on your bed with the entire world of burdens bearing on your back and a heaviness on your chest, and your face wet with tears - these words don't mean anything.

You want to punch the next person that says "it'll all be okay, trust Allah." Like of course, I trust Allah. I know. I get it. I know everything you're about to tell me because I told someone else this advice. I know all the reworded phrases of having patience and tawakkul.

You know it. And Allah knows you know it. That's why He pushes you to the edge. To see if you chose to turn away. If you chose to have the knowledge and still disregard His wisdom. If you chose to use this hardship to face the opposite direction, to stop praying, to stop asking Him, to give up.

So if you know He is the all-knowing. If you know that He loves you more than you love yourself, Al-Wadud. If you know He's As-Samad, the Satisfier of Needs. Al-Muqtadir, the Creator of All Power. Al-Mujeeb, The Responder to Prayer. Al-Hakeem, the Perfectly Wise. Ar-Raqeeb, the Watchful One.

If you know that He is all of this and more. Keep crying. But cry to Him. Don't ever stop pleading with Him. Don't ever give up.

There isn't a hardship in this world worth you giving up Jannah.

— — —

For those of you suffering in the soft murmurs of the night.

For all those times you thought about it.

For all those times you almost did it.

Keep living. Keep going. For every suffering - scream into your pillow saying you'll live. Saying you'll live with your head held high when you walk and low when you pray. You'll live until you've made Him happy. You'll live until you've cleansed your heart. You'll live until you no longer want death because it's an escape, but death because it's the only step remaining until Jannah.

Your hardships can only make you close to Him. But also - they can only solidify your position in the heavens - to build a home near Aasiya, tortured by her prince charming rich husband who did love her originally. A home near Sumaiya, who was stabbed by a spear simply for attesting the oneness of Allah. A home near Maryam, whose name still has rumors spread wide and far, whose virginity still questioned by the masses, whose labor was only aided by a date palm tree.

You want a home near them. Earn it.

Allah is not incapable of making your life easy. But He chose not to. There's a reason for it. Find the reason. Keep living.

the soul in a container:
your self esteem

"Verily, God loves if any of you does a job, he does it with perfection."

I don't know the source for this, but it has similar roots in a hadith in Muslim.

We aren't perfect - of course not - Allah didn't create us in that manner. But we can achieve certain mastery on certain aspects.

For many of us, we are students, we are just knowledge-seekers. As students, I urge you guys to keep this idea in mind. This concept of striving for perfection. Don't give in mediocre work. Don't hand in assignments you know you did hastily. Allah did not create you to be lazy.

Allah only created only ONE version of YOU. So, who are you? Are you mediocre? In your studies at school, in your class, amongst your peers, in your imaan, in your worship. Are you just at the bare minimum? Are you just above average? Where are you?

Push yourselves. You have the potential. Be phenomenal. Become something you can't even dream of becoming. If your goals don't make you scared, make you shudder to your core, make your heart swell up - they aren't good enough. Reach the breaking point - and then surpass it.

So be the A+ students, so memorize Quran, so do thahajjud every day, so get fit, so spend on your loved ones, so do all the things you are "waiting to do when you grow up". Do the things you fear you never can do.

You are the only YOU that exists and ever will exist on this earth. Do the best YOU, be the perfect YOU.

— — —

"Allah created Man the most beautiful of all His creations."

And as I stare at the moon in all of its beauty I wondered to myself.

The moon is beautiful when it is full. It's beautiful when it is half. It's beautiful when it is as thin as a fingernail.

You are more beautiful than the moon.

You are beautiful in all your forms too.

So don't be down. Even when you feel like no one on earth actually finds you beautiful, remember that Allah already told you that you are.

— — —

"The problem is that we underestimate our worth and we lean back to mediocrity, satisfied only with the little effort we put in and not willing to be our best. & then we question why the results of our actions are of poor quality. We're lazy, negative, fussy, disorganized but wearing rose coloured glasses that show us to be better than we are. How foolish are we, to not understand that the problems that arise in life are all due to our problematic selves, underestimating our worth & leaning back to mediocrity. We can do better."

As Muslims sometimes when we think of ourselves we cut slack. I'm a decent Muslim. I'm moderate. I pray 5x. I don't smoke, drink, party, or commit zinna. I fast during the month of Ramadan. I eat halal. Well then I'm all good. I don't need anything else.

Wrong. The point isn't to stay away from Hell. The point is to get into Heaven and get into the highest level of Heaven. We aren't mediocre. We aren't moderate. We are better. We should pray as slow and as perfect as the Sahabas. We should do as much dhikr as possible. We should read Quran daily. We should strive to be near darn perfect. Cause that makes Allah smile. And you want Him to smile. Don't you?

— — —

"Realize what good you have in yourself. Don't just give up on yourself." – Sheikh Abdul Nasir Jangda

Imagine the person you could be. And don't reject the thought. Don't think, oh I could never become a hijabi/niqaabi/thobee or I can never pray on time, so I'll just be a mediocre person. Don't think, I'll never become a hafidh or I'll never really be that religious, so I like being in the middle.

Says who? Who says you can't be the one granted Jannah without questioning. How dare you degrade your own self and create arbitrary lines you never even plan on crossing? You cannot possibly be that arrogant to act as if you can see the future.

Really, the only thing getting in the way of Jannah is you. Your career, your environment, your parents and these matters are all excuses you made for yourself to hold yourself back.

Because really, you're scared you actually can be THAT religious. You're scared that you might actually one day become the people you've always admired. Or maybe you're scared you'll miss the haram things you've been doing once you change.

But really, you are just afraid of your own potential.

And it's time for you to stop and take a deep breath. It is time for you to unleash the love that is inside you and give yourself to your Lord.

— — —

"On the Day of Judgement we are gonna be raised naked. And just like no one is going to have the time to look/care because of the severity of that day and everyone only worried for themselves - we should be that way here. We should not even have the time to look at someone and judge them. And nor should we care about our physical features and be saddened by them." This hits two important points.

1) Judging others: this is an absolute no no in our religion. You are not God. You have no right to judge someone else. Know that even if you are their closest friend, you still don't know their intention. Only God knows that. You might think someone is extremely pious but Allah knows if that person is doing it with sincerity or if they are doing it to show off. He also knows the deepest darkest secrets and sins of everyone. Don't judge the "religious" and don't put them on a pedestal. Don't judge the not-so-practicing and put them under your feet. You are not God. Be busy purifying and bettering yourself. You'll notice that the ones who are truly engrossed in the worship of Allah and have a certain nur - they don't judge. They come with sweet words and gentle hands. They have with them an aura. That anyone

can go up to them and spill secrets and find comfort. I hope all of you are lucky enough to meet a handful of people like that. And become those types of people as well.

2) Saddened by our own image: this is a reminder to myself every single morning and every single night. For every sister and brother struggling with their looks. As they sit and feel like the ugly one in the crew. Our bodies are perishable. It's a container. Treat it with respect and feed it well. But understand that it's temporary. Love every inch of it because Allah created you. And someone will love you from the spaces between your fingers, the cracks on your palm, the edge of your shoulder, to the dent on your temple.

Your worth is in your book that will be handed to you. Not how you look. And not how others view you.

So don't be judgemental. Let people talk because people spread hate about the prophet himself. And focus on that book of yours.

— — —

"How cool is it that the same God that created mountains and oceans and galaxies and puppies, looked at you and thought the world needed one of you too."

I think a lot of us forget our importance to the world. We get lost in our inner sadness, our stress, our smallness.

But the world needs you. Perhaps in a big way, perhaps you're the doctor that's meant to go to third world countries and treat a man who can't afford treatment and in turn give his family the chance to piece their lives together again. Or the lawyer that saves an innocent man from going to jail, or helps a woman get custody of her child. However way your career affects the world - maybe you're meant to do it.

Or maybe in smaller ways. Maybe you're the father who teaches his daughters that their validation comes from God and not from boys. Or the mother who teaches her children a love of memorizing Quran.

Or the friend who brings other friends closer to Allah. Or the friend who prevents their friend from committing suicide. Or the friend who helps a friend get over drug abuse. Or you help someone with heartbreak, eating disorders, depression. And that's how you affect the world. Because your friends need you.

Maybe your duas are the ones getting answered. Maybe you were put here to make duas for others and see how happy it makes them when Allah answers you.

You are important. You are needed.

You are just as important as the moon that controls the tides, and the mountains that peg down the ground, the rain that brings forward sustenance. Allah made you the best of His creations, in the best of forms.

— — —

"For you to take away your sin - you have to have an identity shift." - MD Hasan

I think for those who have changed from being a not so practicing to more practicing to even more practicing Muslim, we see how our identity shifts. We see how we go from someone who misses fajr in the morning to someone who wakes up for fajr every morning to someone who perhaps wakes up for fajr and stays on that rug until duha.

I know for a fact that with that identity shift, many people lose friends. You used to smoke weed, you used to party, you used to go to formals, you used to chill at hookah bars, you used to live the free-mixing life. But when you changed, you realized that you didn't want to do those things. So after bailing so many times there comes a distance. You can't go to your friend's birthdays anymore, you can't chill while they're high. Things change - some people are lucky and their friends get to change with them and it's a climb together - and others have to let go of some friends.

The identity shift can be drastic but most times it is gradual. From tank tops and sleeveless salwar kameez to abayas and niqaab. From blasting kanye to blasting Mishary. These changes can happen - you've seen them happen to your friends and to yourselves.

Change your identity. BECOME that person you are so intimidated to become. "Our deepest fear is not that we are inadequate. Our deepest fear is that we are powerful beyond measure. It is our light, not our darkness that most frightens us. We ask ourselves, Who am I to be brilliant, gorgeous, talented, fabulous? Actually, who are you not to be?"

Who are you not to be the person who DOESN'T watch haraam movies and wastes time on tv. The person who prays 5 times. The person who prays the sunnah portions. The person who prays qiyaam. The person who memorizes the last juz. The person who memorizes the entire Quran. The person who wears hijab/abaya/niqaab. The person who walks away from ill speech. The person who walks away from haraam relationships.

Point two: allow people to change and with that, allow your perception of them to change. This is so important. Just because a brother USE to have girls on his laps and now he's wearing a thobe and praying gives you NO RIGHT to say that he is faking it or bring up his past sins. Just because a girl once flaunted herself but now dons the abaya does not mean you get to say she is doing it to get a guy.

People grow - people make mistakes - people become stronger in their deen because of these mistakes. Think about even the companions of the prophet - they have buckets of sins - they are not sacred intangible beings. Some of the most pious people were people who originally used to pay for prostitutes or have free premarital affairs.

Look forward - at your future self and the future of others - the possibility of everyone having palaces in Jannah. Who are you not to become a mu'min, and who are you to say that they are not true mu'minoon.

— — —

"Don't be envious of someone who has something they wanted, you don't know what Allah took away from them."

We are always comparing ourselves. Our summer vacations, our workloads, our financial situations. We compare our b-roll film to someone else's highlights.

You think someone is going to snapchat their wet pillow, the one they spent the entire night crying on? You think someone is going to instagram the bruises on their mother's back? You think someone is going to facebook their minimum wage paycheck? You think people tweet all the death anniversaries they remember? How would someone show you their old memories. The times they were abused. The times they were sexually harassed. The times their stomach begged for food but couldn't afford to eat. The photos of the broken down apartment they shared with other people. The forgotten birthdays, the hospital visits, the anonymous hate. The xanga posts mocking them, the middle school bullying, the demeaning words echoing. The IV drips, the puking, the scars on their wrist.

We have no idea about other people's battles. The feelings inside our gut that no one else can feel - well, you're not the only one. Other people have those feelings too, probably for complete different reasons. Other people cry their nights and fake their happiness.

It's all a facade. And the only one who knows it all is the All-Seeing. Even the memories you've suppressed, the aches that you've forgotten, the wishes you hold on to. It's all known to Him.

So stop looking around. He knows what He has in store for you, He knows the hardships you and only you can handle. And He knows the same information about all individuals. So look in the palm of your hands or the place of sujood. All your pains should fall on that prayer mat, because He holds all your ease.

— — —

"When you lead someone to the truth - only their ego prevents them from taking it." - Dr. Altaf Husain

We see this most with our siblings - especially if you have younger siblings. You are obviously wiser in many respects and you will push your younger siblings and show them the truth and still they will retort back and not accept your guidance, whether it be religious guidance or academic guidance.

But this is true for our own self. When someone corrects your wudhu, your prayer, your recitation - or when someone tries to advise you on gender relations or controlling the tongue - or, perhaps the one disregarded by many, when someone corrects your hijab. We can almost always see how defensive we get - how quickly we put up a guard, how quickly we dismiss that person's advice. (Granted, they should also do it in a proper manner, not through public facebook posts or in front of your friends) But we still retort back.

We don't practice self-reflection - is what I am doing wrong? How wrong is it? Is Allah happy with me in what I am doing? How do I better myself? Am I just making up excuses when I clearly know the truth?

So next time advice comes, smile, and take it. It could be an angel reminding you of the position Allah wants to take you to.

— — —

"There are prophets who come to Allah on the day of judgement with zero followers. Zero impact. But Allah gives them the highest ranks of Jannah, why? Because of their pursuit, their effort." -- Ustaadh Nouman Ali Khan

It's not about how many rakats you pray a day. It's not about how well you observe hijab. It's not about how many surahs you have memorized.

It's about the effort. Your sincerity. Did you really try?

Because some things are easy for some people - there are hijabis who find wearing hijab easy but praying five times difficult. There are people who find memorizing Quran easy but observing proper hayaa difficult. There are some who find praying easy but wearing hijab difficult.

Allah tests everyone differently - with wealth, with family, with faith, with school, with hayaa, with the opposite gender, with drugs and alcohol and haraam food and pornography.

You know if you're being sincere in your efforts to excel. Don't fool yourself. Be honest, how hard are you trying to get into His paradise. How hard are you trying to improve? What obstacles are you actually attempting to overcome. What have you been postponing. What excuses have you been collecting.

Are you really working towards more modesty in your attire? Are you really trying to get your prayers on time? Are you really cutting off pornography? Are you really attempting to quit smoking?

Allah knows the deepest crevice in your heart. He's the one who made it. So be honest in your efforts, and push yourself harder. No one is where they can potentially be. Everyone can be better, everything has room for improvement.

— — —

"We don't even know our capacity - ibadah is set up to show us our capacity." - Sheikh Muhammad ibn Faqih

You might think - really? Am I really going to be that person who prays five whole times a day? Every single day. For the rest of my life? That's a lot of prayers. Am I really going to be able to wake up before sunrise and pray fajr every single day? Can I actually read Quran every single day? Will I ever be able to really memorize any more than I already have. Can I actually quit smoking and hookah and the party life. Will I actually have the time to pray sunnah for the rest of my life. Is qiyaam really something I can achieve on a regular basis?

But you'll never know unless you implement it. You don't know what you were made to do. Yes there are people who are successful in school and in practicing their deen and in being a social butterfly. They exist.

Baby steps are fine. But you should always be pushing. Always be moving forward. Stop saying one day. Say no- today. Today is the day. Right now is your chance.

Push the limits you set for yourself. Push the limits Shaytaan keeps setting for you.

You might be that person. With 4.0 and thahajjud and qiyaam and chapters of Quran everyday. And you might look at yourself and think whoa how do I even do this.

You might just become the person Allah enters into Jannah - free of questioning, free of blame. Just saying to you "enter my paradise".

— — —

No matter how many deeds a believer does, he is never satisfied. And a person of weak faith feels sufficient in whatever he does.

That's why the sahabas did so much. Even after being promised Jannah by the Prophet himself, they continuously did every good deed they possibly could.

But we pray 5 times and tap ourselves in the back.

A page of Quran a day seems impressive to some of us. But some of your own friends might actually be reading an hour or more of Quran a day, finishing it every few weeks.

Praying the sunnah portions of prayers is more than enough for some of us. Even then we struggle with the sunnah for duhr and the sunnah ghair muakadah for isha.

Listening to lectures seems to be reserved for physical events we go to on Fridays, but your friends are listening to something at least once a day or spending their weekend reviewing seminars or reading hadiths and tafseer.

When your Duas aren't being answered - don't become frustrated. Maybe Allah wants you to become the person that prays day and night. Maybe praying 5 + Duha + Awabeen isn't enough. Maybe He knows you are capable of more. Maybe He expects your hour of qiyaam and more than four rakats of thahajjud.

You have no idea what you are capable of until you start doing it.

Your worship is immeasurable. That's why the reward is immeasurable. You cannot possibly quantify it.

— — —

"A lot of people die full. Full of their dreams, full of their talent, full of ideas, full of skills, full of intelligence, and abilities that they never reached for. They never tapped. They never got into. They never used it. But you know something, you're not in a graveyard - yet. And we get one life. And every passing moment - we will never get back again." -- Motivational Talk on Youtube

You have so much potential, you can't even fathom it. If only you could see the neurons in your brain that light up. They way your brain continues to work whether you are awake or you are asleep. The way your heart never stops pumping.

But you get to decide what you leave on this earth and what you take with you.

So try to leave behind a legacy - it may be a legacy written down in history books: a scientist that found a cure, a lawyer that fought for justice, a surgeon naming a surgical method, an engineer advancing the world - or a legacy for a handful of people: a teacher that inspired, a mother ever generous, a friend forever thoughtful. And each step - every moment - you are a second closer to your goal. So every exam is for you to get there - to the end, to the finish line, to your epitome.

And remember to take with you your deeds - the handful of tasbeeh, the nightly recitation of al-ikhlaas and mulk, the extra two raka'at at night or a tad before noon, the reviewing of Allah's words on your tongue, the small acts of charity, the kind words to a friend.

And even when the world isn't working your way - remember that time is not in your hands, and your akhira is so close by.

And He is the best of planners. So let Him write your story, but keep turning the page, let the ink fill it up.

— — —

"For what it's worth: It's never too late to be whoever you want to be. I hope you live a life you're proud of, and if you find that you're not, I hope you have the strength to start over."

F. Scott Fitzgerald

You decide who you want to be. How studious you want to be, how popular you want to be, how practicing you want to be.

It's like the "editing phase" of life. (Reference to Sh. Yaser Birjas's Love Notes Al Maghrib Class) Take out things that aren't bringing meaning into your life. Stop taking classes that make you upset. Stop watching shows that dumb your mind. Stop being with people who make you cry. And add things - be it prayer, be it fasting, be it reading Surah Al-Mulk before bed, be it a hobby you used to have - like reading books, jump roping, basketball, be it elements of a healthier lifestyle like going to the gym or cooking wholesome food and packing lunches.

Learn more about yourself and become someone you are comfortable with. Being comfortable with your skin. With your body (yes, that's probably the hardest, especially if you've suffered with self esteem issues forever). With your intellect. With your habits. With your smile.

You might not find that place - but get somewhere where you aren't crying every night, where you don't feel insufficient, where you can feel Allah being happy with your efforts, where you can imagine telling your children, "this is how your mom/dad was in college". Become someone you would admire yourself.

Become satisfied with the parts of you that have hurt before. Become satisfied with your efforts.

"As for he who gives and fears Allah and believes in the best [reward], we will ease him towards ease." - Surah Al-Layl

Once you start, He will only make it easier.

Sounds impossible to be fasting and praying and reading Quran and doing work and studying for exams and being healthy. All the good in this world, how can one person have it all?

Because - Allah. Not you. He gives it. He makes it easy. & No matter how far you go - fall of the edge of the earth - and commit every major sin, from zinna to drugs - if you decide to come back, Allah welcomes you. Eradicating your sins as if nothing ever happened.

His mercy is overwhelming.

— — —

"You think on the Day of Judgement, he [Ibn Majud] is gonna say, 'Yeah Allah this is all great but I wish I could have been a little taller in the dunya'. You think he cares? You think it matters to him at all?" -Sheikh Omar Suleiman | Body Image: Reality and Standards.

I think this is a huge problem for many girls. It's a long process to eventually be okay with our body. Even people who you think might be okay with their body, are probably not as okay as they seem. And of course it's not limited to sisters. I'm sure brothers out there have issues and yes, anorexia exists on the boys side too.

So really, if you are having a hard time. Refer back to Surah At-Tin and its tafseer. And how Allah did not simply create us, but He perfected us in our mold, He fashioned us. To be upset with our body means to be upset with Him.

And that itself is a test. How grateful are you?

— — —

"There are girls who had acid thrown on their face wishing - praying that they had just an ounce of your beauty. Just a fraction of the beauty that you have, that you're ungrateful for." - Omar Shareef

Body image and self esteem, a long war with battles galore. On some days it's fine, on other days you're bawling your eyes as you knock out.

It's not just for girls - boys have the issue too. Except we don't call it "starving" when boys do it - we call it "cutting".

This body is so temporary. What does it have? 40 years? 60? 80? How many years does it have to "look good" because it won't stay looking that appealing forever.

Not that you shouldn't take care of it - it has a haqq upon you - feed it well, exercise it well, keep it going.

But these subjective ideas of beauty - the collar bones, the jawline, the height, the hair - they're not things we should be upset over.

Ask Al-Musawwir, the fashioner of forms, to shape you the way you see beauty.

When you see the moon ask Allah to give you beauty like that of the moon He created. Or a portion of that beauty. Or at least enough of it so that you can look in the mirror and feel radiant.

And be satisfied, for He hasn't tested you with a "deformity". And start prepping for the day where none of it will matter. Where no beauty can save you from walking the bridge over darkness.

— — —

"Reinvent yourself as many times as you want."

To the person who pray five times, to the person who prays on time, to the person who prays sunnah, to the person who prays nafl, to the person who prays thahajjud, to the person who prays qiyaam and then fajr and then stays on that prayer rug until duha.

To the person who fasts on Mondays and Thursdays.

To the person who reads an ayah of Quran a day, to the person who reads a page of Quran a day, to a person who reads a surah or two from the Quran after fajr, to the person who reads a juzz of Quran a day.

To the person who curses less, to the person who doesn't curse at all, to the person whose tongue is in constant remembrance and glorification of Allah.

To the person who watches less entertainment, to the person whose eyes can't see certain entertainment, to the person whose love for entertainment vanishes.

To the person who is grateful of their parents, to the person who is immediately obedient to their parents, to the person who enters Jannah because of their obedience to their parents.

To the person who studies sometimes, to the person who studies often, to the person who is habitually studying even when there are no exams.

To the person who eats well, to the person who eats healthy, to the person who exercises, to the person who lives a beautiful holistic lifestyle.

You wake up and decide what kind of person you want to be.

And it's okay if you weren't the person in your dreams.

That's what the sun is for - to rise again so Allah wakes you anew.

swimming
in serenity:
salaah

"Salaah and Zakat are always the first two pillars to be sent to the people." - Sh. Omar Suleiman - Marked for Greatness | Surah Maryam Part 2

It's kind of crazy the importance people will give to secondary things. Hijab is very important, but it isn't as important as Salaah.

I am in no way promoting that you should fix your salaah first before observing hijab - that's actually how shaytaan gets you to take away your own good deeds, by telling you to do things in an arbitrary chronological order.

I am stating that you cannot simply be a good Muslim and think it's sufficient. You cannot wear abaya and think you're good. You cannot give up haraam entertainment and think you'll get to Jannah. You cannot just memorize Quran and feel like Allah will give you those robes.

The first thing you're asked about isn't going to be - did you wear hijab properly or did you tend to your parents or did you tell the truth or did you recite Quran regularly or did you fast. These are all important things, these are all responsibilities, but these aren't the things you are questioned about first.

The first thing is salaah. You fix salaah - five times a day - ON TIME - because not doing it on time is basically handing in a half done assignment late to the professor without even apologizing but still expecting an A.

No one has perfected this. None of us have this pillar down. You can pray all five prayers, include all portions of the sunnah and nafl and use the longest of surahs - and it still might not be accepted, it still might not be enough because you lacked concentration.

You want to be better? You want to change? Reading and listening to lectures and going the next step and wearing hijab and niqaab is great - but if you don't have the first thing Allah asked for - what do you have?

Are you ready to go empty handed? Or do you have some scraps of torn paper of some random prayers. Late assignments. Crumpled paper with gum on them. Papers with half sentences and sentence fragments. Papers with coffee stains and burnt edges. A nice piece of stock paper with glitter on it from that one laylatul qadr. Another strong neatly typed single space paper from the time you needed something desperately.

Imagine if all the thoughts you had during your salaah were written down - the lyrics you accidentally thought of, the outfits you planned, the homework you finally understand, the to-do list that crept into your mind, the text message you just read, the email you haven't sent, the instagram post you haven't posted, the dinner you craved - the most erratic thoughts all written down - and every few thoughts later you said "Allahu Akbar - Allah is Greater" and didn't actually mean it because if you thought He was, you would only be thinking of Him.

— — —

"You may not ask Allah for water, but do you need it? Yes. A disbeliever doesn't ask Allah for water, but he needs it. Whether he believes it or not, he still needs Allah. When he is asking for water, he is actually asking from the source. The air is being supplied by Allah, and you need Him whether you realize it or not." - from Tafseer of Surah Ar-Rahmam, Ustaadh Nouman Ali Khan

My aunts asked me to find out why my cousins stopped praying on purpose. So I asked them frankly, and they said it was because they kept asking Allah for things and He wasn't giving it to them. I think this is a recurring reason among young teens that kind of stays with them and so when things don't go their way, they refuse to pray. They are angry with Allah. "Why does He want us to pray if He won't even answer? I prayed so hard for this thing and I didn't get it."

But who are you to be angry with the Creator of the world? The One who created you.

Allah is in no need of your prayers. So by you refusing to pray, you're only harming yourself.

Your refusal to pray does not lower Allah's majesty or greatness.

All it does is dock points off your scale of deeds, all it does is keep you friends with shaytaan, all it does it darken your heart so it's harder to do other good deeds.

Lectures on duas being accepted can be found, I recommend everyone to see why their duas aren't being accepted, or to realize that maybe Allah will grant them later on or maybe He has a better plan.

But that's no reason to stop praying. Even if you're upset and frustrated, just keep praying. Even if you feel nothing, keep praying.

You don't know which two rakats will save you on that horrifying results day.

— — —

You are not special because you are fasting. People fast for days, for several reasons, some religious, some secular. Fasting is not what makes you Muslim.

What makes you a believer is your salaah. The first thing you will be questioned about. So those who don't have the five prayers down, fix that. You are on thin ice. And Allah is waiting for when you'll call Him.

"The difference between us and them is salaah. Whoever neglects it is a kaafir." (Ahmad)

And for those who are feeling content that they have the five prayers down, don't be so content. We have all made mistakes in our prayers. You're about to head out, so you rush. You're praying during halftime or some commercial break, so you rush. You barely know if you did 4 rakats or just 2. You probably can't even recall the surahs you recited. You were overhearing the side conversation that went on during prayer. You've missed prayer times and made them up at night. There was a song stuck in your head while you prayed. You thought of your homework or what you'll eat for dinner, while you were standing in front of the Lord of the universe.

You cannot possibly say that you have prayed all of your prayers with perfect focus. So really, we should all be very wary, and very concerned.

And that's why we should do nafl. All the nafls we can possibly find.

74

If you're sitting around groaning after maghrib, get up and do nafl. If you're tempted to watch a movie to "kill a few hours before iftaar", do some nafl. If you're suffering from insomnia, do some nafl. Even if you don't FEEL the connection with Allah, do it anyway. Think of it as extra credit. So when your deeds are being weighed, and the angels are explaining each of your prayers, and there are missing prayers, faulty prayers, incomplete prayers - they can look over to your extra credit and tack on the points.

Imagine, one lazy Sunday you prayed just two rakats of nafl with the two shortest surahs you know - and that was what saved you from the blazing fire of hell.

— — —

So imagine every beautiful thing you have ever seen in your life.

The places you've traveled to, the hotels you've been to.

The sunrises and sunsets, pink skies and perfect blue-no-cloud-in-sight skies, waterfalls, lakes, perfectly crisp burnt orange fall leaves, blushing pink cherry blossoms, glowing incandescent stars sprawled across the sky, the water droplet stuck on an emerald green leaf, the rainbow puddle at the edge of the sidewalk, the intricate snowflake on your scarf, the flickering of a candle in a still room, times square at night, the Eiffel tower glittering, the view from a skyscraper, the sky from a country-side veranda. No-filter-needed, instagram worthy pictures that snapchat doesn't do justice to.

And beautiful people, whose face glows without highlighter.

Every single beautiful phenomenon, from heart surgeries to deep sea diving. Think about every moment you were at an utter loss of words.

Now listen to this: "The two Rak'ah before the Fajr prayer are better than this world and all it contains." (Sahih Muslim)

So you can claim to pray five times a day - but if you're praying fajr consistently after the appointed time is gone, you're missing out on the reward of something unimaginable.

It would only take you about 10-15 minutes to wake up and pray and then go back to your warm bed. Are you really giving up akhira for a few hours of sleep?

___ ___ ___

"Don't tell me you're ready to do anything for the Deen, when you can't even bench press a blanket for fajr." - Mike Tyson

How many of you are part of Islamic organizations? How many of you are MSA Board Members? How many of you give out flyers at your masjids promoting Al-Maghrib classes? How many of you are part of MUNA, YM, MAS, ISNA, ICNA, and the tons of organizations out there? How many of you are leaders of your halaqas?

Now tell me - how many of you pray fajr on time?

Don't expect Allah to help you do dawah work and work for this deen if you can't even fulfill one of the five pillars of Islam. Don't expect Him to benefit you in any way - if you can't even fulfill His minimal request.

Think about what Allah sees the next time you're in front of a group of people explaining what Taqwa is or giving a Khutbah on gender relations. He sees a disobedient servant trying to get others to obey His laws.

___ ___ ___

"Struggle with no goal in front of you. Struggle as is worthy of Allah."

Struggle as is worthy of Allah - in all sections of life. Not just spiritual struggling of praying on time or praying qiyam-al-layl, but also struggling in your own behavior and character. Making yourself better, happier, more helpful. Struggling in your work ethics - time management, organization. Struggling in your studies and making sure you study hard enough.

This life shouldn't be a waste - do all of it as is worthy of Allah.

Does Allah deserve your haphazard prayers? Does He deserve the slapdash paper you handed in after He enabled you to get an education? Does He deserve the lackadaisical manner by which you interact with your parents?

He created us with such care, He deserves more than the few minutes we give Him, and the careless manner by which we live our lives.

— — —

"I can't pray fajr - but you can get up that early if you had a flight to catch - it's just that there isn't enough reason for you." - MD Hasan

Is waking up for the one who created the heavens and the earth - not a good enough reason? Don't even do the four rakat - just 2 rakats - is that so much for Him to be asking of you.

Honestly, the things we do for this dunya - the all nighters, the way we harm our body with sleep deprivation and over exertion, the crazy hours we work standing on our feet, the money sacrifices we make to "fit in" (even in the smallest ways, like buying starbucks when a regular cup of coffee would work the same).

But after just the sunnah prayers, we get lazy. Like why bother with the nawafil.

So when you're feeling lazy, always remember. The words in the voice of the man whose footsteps could be heard in Paradise: Hasten to prayer. Hasten to success. Prayer is better than sleep.

— — —

"Your imaan is your greatest treasure. Take account of it. Value it. Build it."

We work so hard sharpening our other skills: ace-ing our academic world, getting better at poetry, learning art, learning software, learning lab techniques, increasing strength through lifting, cooking, baking, a world of things.

Sometimes we are diligent in practicing these things, we know that it'll be useful in our careers or in our life. Sometimes we are lazy and rely on pure talent.

But imaan falls under the boat. It's the last thing we think of building. Because most of us feel like we have it. We believe and that's it.

When you need a high, you'll go to a lecture or watch something on youtube.

But of all the things that matter - imaan matters the most. It's not just about praying and calling it a day. It's about feeling prayer, about khushoo in prayer not being reserved for once in a blue moon. It's about understanding the Quran we recite. It's about perfecting the recitation of it. It's about knowing stuff, feeling stuff, making it so strong that you can identify when shaytaan is getting to you and you can block him out. Making it so strong that neither hardships nor ease will make you falter.

— — —

"Happiness is in the heart. And Allah owns the hearts." - Ustaadh Mohammad Elshinaway

So why would you expect to find it anywhere else.

It's is not the movies and music and food that gives you happiness. It won't be a boy or girl or a dream job.

You can have everything in the world and not find that happiness you were searching for.

Happiness is really a byproduct.

And do you think that the One who created the water - the kind that causes destructions like tsunamis, the kind that is peaceful like a quiet lake, the kind that is sweet like springs, and the kind inside your own body. The One who literally molded every ventricle, artery, atrium, & gives the heart the unbelievable power to pump blood all over the body - that Creator - can't figure out who you are?

Is it you who created your own soul or Allah the one who fashioned it. Is it you who knows better for your own soul or the Creator.

Think of how much of an insult it is. Imagine a scientist created a robot, and then the robot thinks it can reprogram itself and fix it with different things. The creator would know the creation well enough to know what to give it and how to fix it.

So trusting in Him. For happiness and contentment.

If five years of thahajjud isn't enough, do five more. If you think a week of praying 5 times and asking for something means He should give it - you're crazy. And if you've been doing qiyaam for a week it means you are capable of doing it for a month or so.

There are so many ways to get what you want. You can only ask Him for things anyways.

So don't waste wishes on stars and pennies in fountains. Where's your thahajjud?

— — —

"Sometimes Allah isn't giving you what you want because He misses seeing you in the night prayer." - Sh Waleed Basyouni

Whatever it is that you want: stop saying Allah isn't answering you.

You didn't make Dua long enough. You didn't make it hard enough.

You didn't spend every night waking up for thahajjud, using the longest Surahs you know and the staying in sujood literally begging Him for it.

You didn't cry in the rain asking Him for it. You didn't fast (nafl) a whole week and beg for it each time you broke your fast.

If you want something bad enough - you'll do all this and more. And more. And more.

On that note - if you can pull all nighters for finals, waking up at 5AM for two or four quick rakats of thahajjud will only benefit you.

Ask Him. He's waiting.

— — —

"[Before prophethood, Muhammad SAW would go to the cave and contemplate] This was at the peak of his life. He had everything. He had no financial needs. He had children. He had a beautiful marital life. He was not at a vulnerable position. He only went to the cave for Allah." - Sh. Omar Suleiman □

We often find ourselves turning to Allah in times of need.

Financial needs, academic needs, family problems, heartbreak.

That's when the sujood gets longer, that's when the nawafil fasting starts, that's when we start thahajjud, that's when we take out our Quran.

But the sign of a true believer is that the worship - it's the same, when Allah afflicts with hardship and when Allah bestows blessings.

You don't worship Allah on your timeline. Worship isn't a magic button for you to press and reap rewards, for you to make dua and see it appear in front of your eyes.

You don't simply pray a whole night when you're breaking into pieces. You also pray the nights when you're relieved; when you're happy.

It's worship out of loving Allah. It's something you feel - and until you've felt it, you'll never know what that "taste" of worship is. And if you've ever felt it - you know you want it back.

You might procrastinate your papers and your studying and your work deadlines and your weight goals. Don't procrastinate falling in love with Allah.

What if you don't get to taste it. What if life slips away from you and you never get that feeling again.

And that opportunity of seeing the One who created you gets snatched from you.

— — —

"If you die tonight - will you care that you have homework to finish or cooking to finish or a basketball game you have to watch or a tv show or whatever it is that people keep themselves busy with. Even important things - would you care?" (Referring to praying as if it's your last prayer) Dr. Farhan Abdul Azeez

Would you care about all those things or would answering your Lord be more important? Would you start caring about your prayers? If you did them - if you did them well.

People will be begging Allah for just one more chance - one more chance to bow down to Him in this world.

You are here now. You still get to bow down now.

How do you call yourself a Muslim if you have not fulfilled a main pillar of Islam? How can you know that the difference between a believer and a disbeliever is in the salaah and still not pray?

How can you pick up the call of friends and bosses and keep up with tv shows and homework but not answer the call of the one who fashioned you in perfection. Of the one who sends down the rain and clothes you and feeds you. How do you reject His call, 5 times a day?

Your name is on the Angel of Death's checklist. You have no idea when you'll be gone. Make sure all your affairs are sorted. Make sure you have the answer to the first question you will be asked on the Day of Judgement. Make sure you have the prayers and make sure they are well done. And if you're sure your past self didn't do them properly, then make sure you have enough nawafil to cover for those insufficient prayers.

A believer is never satisfied with his worship, he is always doing more. Are you a believer. The one that the angels make dua for?

— — —

"Wastabbur: worship and be patient. Don't just "try out" the deen." - Sh. Omar Suleiman | Marked for Greatness; Surah Maryam Part 2

You cannot pray all night for something and expect it to happen the next day. You cannot pray extra prayers all week long and then say that Allah didn't give you what you wanted.

You don't just pray fajr on time once and then magically expect to get an A on the exam.

It's not a magic button.

There are people whose Duas come true consistently. But if you ask about them, they all have one thing in common. They are constantly asking.

This means that not only are they praying, they are also doing dhikr or talking to Allah or reading Quran.

The time you fill up with shows and games and Facebook, they fill it up with qiyaam and Quran.

So of course Allah will answer their requests. He feels shy to return hands empty.

So become one of those people. So connected with Allah that it is like magic.

Maryam had fruits inside her room, fruits that weren't in season, fruits she didn't grow or buy. It was the most generous Allah that provided her.

Miracles can happen. It's just up to you how close you want to be with Him, the giver of miracles.

& the first step might be thahajjud (after you have all 5 down)

And after that it's all about the patience. A beautiful patience.

— — —

"It is You we worship and You we ask for help."

Every single one of you recites this ayah several times a day. And even if you don't pray at all - every single one of you has this ayah memorized.

But you forget the profound meaning of it. It is only Allah we worship and it is ONLY He who can help us.

If you pray with khushoo and really, I mean really really, interact with your prayer, your body would tremble when you recite this.

It is literally only He who can change the current state. Everything else is really just us trying really hard - the medicine, the studying, the working out. But at the end of the day it is up to Allah to help you. And you can only get so much from the creation - because all of this - every piece of land in all the planets, every star, and every moon - it's all part of His dominion. So who else would have the power to change anything.

So whatever it may be - changing you from someone not so practicing into someone practicing, changing your parents hearts and softening them, changing your GPA, or changing the status of someone's heart - it is not dependent on anything but Allah.

He is the turner of hearts and He turns your heart just as He turns others hearts. He can turn hearts towards each other and towards Him.

Only He can wake you up in the morning - so why turn to things to help you feel better - why turn to music and movies and cigarettes.

He made your heart. Give Him His right. Let Him rule it too.

And maybe the best way to do that is through long qiyaam and long thahajjuds. Every time you need Him.

— — —

Once, I was with a friend and I had not prayed isha yet but I figured I would go home and pray instead of praying at college.

And then she said "No. You should pray now."

I was taken aback and slightly confused because isha prayer has a long time spectrum. I would be home in an hour or so - I'd still have a good few hours to pray isha. I'd be able to shower and relax a little before praying. So I insisted we get going home. And then she said:

"What if we don't get home. You'd face Allah with this salaah missing."

That thought never crossed my mind. And I swear I got scared. She was absolutely right.

We procrastinate things thinking we have so much time. But if we continue with our bad habits, and we continue saying "inshaAllah one day, I'll do this and this.

But at the end of all these "hopefully, one day, inshaAllah" - we will face Allah with a battered up book - gaps everywhere, missing salaahs and incomplete salaahs, sins upon sins we forgot to seek forgiveness for, nullified good deeds due to our tongues, memories of heedlessness, hours of wasted time.

Praying isn't a chore to wipe off a list - it serves so many purposes. And one of them is to gain perspective. A world that's far bigger than you.

There's a house in Jannah with your name on it.

You don't need to slave hours over at a desk, deal with loans and paperwork, have taxes rip off half your paycheck, miss socializing and sacrifice family time. All the things you need to do to get a decent home in this world - you don't need to do any of those things to get the palace in Jannah.

You just need to get to Jannah.

— — —

"Regardless of if you feel the high or don't. Worship is about Allah, not the high." -Yasmin Mogahed

In the beginning of our journey towards Islam, like the moment when we first start practicing and really getting into it - we go through this high. This high is a phase. It doesn't last long. We go down on our iman and sometimes up again. But we aren't supposed to chase the high and only be religious during those fleeting moments. It's good to want the high, the high will rejuvenate us. But the high shouldn't be the only motivation for us to worship. And the five basic prayers certainly does not fall into that category.

The five prayers is a must. A pillar of our religion. You don't STOP praying when you don't feel the high. You don't STOP praying when you are praying like a zombie. You try harder.

Shaytaan doesn't need to get the people who are already disbelievers - he already has them twisted around his fingertips. They already listen to him. He wants you. You - the one who tries to worship Allah - he wants you. That was his vow to Allah. You are his prize to be strayed from the path. Don't let him do that. Be stronger than that. Pray no matter what - not even if you did do "crazy sins". Pray because it's a fundamental basic aspect of our religion. Pray because Allah told you to.

— — —

"The quality of your entertainment will have an effect on the quality of your worship"- Tariq Ramadan

Have you ever tasted the sweetness of Salaah? Not the power of a salaat where you were begging for something, but a more beautiful salaah, where you didn't have much to ask for but had a wave of contentment pass through you?

It's possible to have that sweetness five times a day. And really, entertainment has such a big effect. If you don't believe me - try it out. Do an experiment, don't watch any tv for a week and don't listen to any music. See how productive you become and see how salaah changes.

One of the reasons we can be blocked from having kushoo in our prayer is our sins placing burden on us. And sometimes, especially in our times, we don't even realize when we are sinning. There are things in tv shows that have become so normalized, I mean, bikinis don't seem to bother us and just a little bit of kissing seems to be okay. So much so that even the younger generation tv shows have so much of it. But it's the small things, the topics discussed in these tv shows that are turning into background murmurs for us. We forget that our ears should not hear the filth of profanity or the hayaa-less conversations. We forget that our eyes shouldn't see other people's awrahs, that "lowering gaze" isn't only for real life but for entertainment too.

But really - how do you expect God to give you peace when you fill your day with more minutes of garbage than those of worship.

— — —

"Subhan comes from the same root of sibaha or to swim. You swim so that you don't drown. When you stop glorifying Allah, you drown in the dunya." - Dr. Farhan Abdul Azeez

This can have two meanings:

1) You drown yourself in the matters of the dunya. You become so engrossed into your daily activities - be it unnecessary things like being so involved with a tv show, or be it good things like your academic life or career.

2) You "drown" in the world and don't actually succeed to your full possible potential - maybe by being unproductive or maybe just by being ungrateful.

See, just because you pray 5 times a day and say the word subhan in rukoo' and sujood - does not mean you actually glorify Allah. If you did it mindlessly, like the way you breath or the way you blink your eyes - it isn't consciously glorifying Him.

Praying 5 times a day does not constitute as you having a good relationship with Allah. Having or attempting to increase your kushoo does.

So learn the ways you already glorify Him:

Subhana rabbi al a'la

Glory to my Lord, the most high.

This is what you are saying every time you place your forehead to the lowest position you can.

You know, if someone asked you to do rukoo' to them - you wouldn't. Not even sujood but rukoo'. But then why are we lazy when we do it? Why don't we do it with full vigilance and awareness and strength. Who are you doing rukoo' to and why do you do it?

You don't have to. No one is putting a gun to your head and forcing you.

So why. Why do you have to glorify Him? Why do you have to swim?

Because the final destination isn't this world and you're swimming through this mess to get there.

loving
the
Quran

Loving the Quran

"Quran is the thing that enables you to see" – AbdulRahman Murphy on Surah Ad-Duha

The Prophet was discontent with the way society was and would go to meditate long before he was even given prophethood. Then after, the Quran came down. It is a book of guidance, like light guiding you through a tunnel.

If the Quran is that book, and this life is a test, then this life is nothing but an OPEN BOOK TEST.

Now it's up to us - do we use the book, or do we not? Do we build a relationship with it, do we read it often, do we touch it, do we hold it, do we understand it?

— — —

Surah Infitar, Ayah 2: And when the stars/planets have fallen and scattered apart - dispersing.

The Surah talks about the Day of Judgement. The scariest day ever possible. But it's amazing how eloquent Allah is in this book. Describing a horrific moment in an intricate, beautiful manner.

There are many words to explain dispersion, and they're each used slightly differently in the Quran: intathara, istatara, infada, intashara, inbatha/imbatha.

In this sentence however, He uses Antatharat, which means fallen off due to a sudden jerking movement. The ayah before this ayah, talks about the sky ripping apart.

Imagine a cloth with pearls on it, if it is suddenly jerked - the pearls fall off it suddenly. This is the image Allah is giving us of the sky being ripped open across, and the stars falling off suddenly.

[This is from Ustaadh Nouman Ali Khan's Tafseer of Surah Infitar]

It's crazy how much is involved in just one verse. You can write PhD Dissertation papers on just one ayah - even just this one ayah, about its etymology and sentence structure and linguistic patterns. We have access to this book - a book with stories and miracles and reminders. And the book literally just sits there, until Ramadan.

Why not open it up? Why not read it? Explore it. Listen to tafseers. Immerse yourself into just one verse, or maybe find a surah you love and go deep deep into it. You'll come to tears at Allah's glory and majesty. Do it. I dare you.

———

Iblis cried loudly four times, first when Allah declared him as cursed, second when he was thrown out, third when Prophet (saw) was born and fourth when Surah Al-Fatiha was revealed [Ibn Kathir in Al Bidayah].

I think we all can understand the importance of Surah Al-Fatiha. It was the first completed surah to be revealed, its significance can be found in countless hadiths, and it's one of the first surahs we were ever taught.

So we recite this surah at minimum, seventeen times a day. We can recite it SUPER DUPER fast too huh? We've definitely become experts on reciting it fast. And most of us probably think we know the translation of it too. But the reality is that we don't REALLY know the translation. Because if we knew the translation, and we really connected and absorbed the translation, we would be scared to be reciting it so fast.

It's a Surah in which we ask Allah for guidance, for not letting us be amongst the people who have angered Him. Yet we recite it super fast. It's almost insulting when we do that. Like we are asking Him to guide us, but we are impatient and doing it really fast because we have better things to do. It's like asking parents for money but doing it super fast so it's like "give me money". And we are also probably thinking of other things while asking for this guidance too.

Let's take "finding khushoo in prayer" one step at a time. And with baby steps, maybe we can hope to be of the people Allah guides. And the first baby step - memorize and understand the words of Surah Al-Fatiha, and recite it SLOWLY in prayer, and while we recite, let's think also about the translation.

— — —

Joke: Three guys wanted to marry the Imaam's daughter, so all three went to the Imaam's house to ask for his daughter's hand in marriage. The Imaam asks the first guy "What's your name?" and he replies "Ibrahim." So the Imaam asks the first guy to recite Surah Ibrahim. And so he does. The Imaam then asks the second guy "What's your name?" to which he replies "Yusuf." And the Imaam asks him to recite Surah Yusuf and so he does. Finally, the Imaam asks the third guy "What's your name?" and the third guy says "My name is Yaseen but people call me qul huwa allah hu ahad."
"95% of the Muslims today are people of 'qul huwa allah'" - Br. Zakir Ahmed

Majority of us have a handful of surahs memorized. The four quls, perhaps al-asr, kawthar, maun, masad, fil. If you open up the mushaf, the physical Quran, you'll see that the surahs you have memorized are only about three pages of the entire book.

Now, no one said you must become a hafidh, but why only have that little memorized? Why be forced to recycle the same surahs in your prayer. Why not have an abundance of surahs that you can pick and choose from.

If you can memorize song lyrics - you can memorize a few lines that your God sent down to you. For, "That chest which does not have any Quran in it is like an abandoned house." Songs by pop stars who themselves have a million heartaches, hindi songs objectifying women, swears sent down by shaytan, do those lyrics have a higher place in your heart than the book of Allah?

Don't memorize to become a hafidh. Memorize because you love Allah, and you love hearing His words uttered through your voice.

— — —

"Indeed, Allah will not change the condition of a people until they change what is in themselves."

Let's say we really want to change but have no clue where to start. Firstly, I think everyone would say - start by praying your daily prayers. Let's say you have that step down. But you still aren't "feeling" it - that spiritual connection or even that conversation with God - feeling.

I think the next logical step would be to connect with the Quran. Just start reading it. Or maybe you're of the group that doesn't "feel" it through recitation, perhaps you really just want to understand and fall in love with the Quran - but these dry translations just don't suffice.

So here's the action plan. Pick a surah you already know. A small, baby one. And research the bajeezus out of it. I mean seriously - RESEARCH it. Like download tafseers about that surah from any speaker and just learn it. Engross yourself in it. You'll discover things - things you had no idea about! Stories you've never heard before! And truly, you'll see the verses in a whole new light inshaAllah .

— — —

"Know your rank with Allah by looking at the rank of the words of Allah in your life" - Farhan Abdul Azeez

There are many of us who go through this series of months where we're busy with school and praying five times and think that we're all good, Allah loves us. We do MSA work and we pray all five, so we're doing everything He asked us to do, right? So we should be up there, like on the scale of good people, because after all, we aren't clubbing and drinking and we aren't disbelievers.

But we barely read the Quran. I mean we read it during Ramadan of course. But barely touch it all the other times. We might listen to it and we might read translations of it and of course we recite the surahs we know. But how much do we engage with this book. This sacred, magnificent, miracle.

Allah's words should be immersed into our lives. It should be the air we breathe, the food we eat. We should be listening to them. Thinking about them. Researching them. (No seriously, RESEARCHING, if you can somehow write a paper about an ayah's translation for school - you'd be getting school work done and gaining Islamic knowledge - trust me, I've done it for sociology, anatomy, religion, media, women & gender studies.) Bring the Quran into your daily life. One ayah a day. One ayah a week even. One the way to school, on the way to work, right after Isha. Whenever there is five minutes to spare (there's always five minutes to spare, I mean you're on facebook ...), use it to engage with the words of Allah.

— — —

"Imagine, on that day. The book that was supposed to testify for you, testifies against you?"

Which means that just because you memorized the Quran or recited it constantly, doesn't mean it'll actually protect you.

No, see, someone who has Quran in their heart, as their best companion, also lives by it. Which means they walk away from vain speech and vulgarity and profanity and gossip. Which means they humble themselves consistently. Which means they talk to their parents with respect. They dress the way Allah asked them to. They interact with the opposite gender the way Allah commanded them to. They don't tell white lies, or cheat on exams. They don't watch the filth they aren't supposed to watch. They lower their gaze.

It's difficult - of course. Or why would the reward be MORE than anything imaginable on this earth. I mean, the reward - it's not just wildest dreams or luxury and comfort but even more. So if the reward is of that caliber, the test must be difficult. It's up to us to decide - so we do our best to pass the test, or do we get lazy and just hope Allah forgives?

I say let's do our best and then hope Allah gives a huge curve because we will definitely need it.

— — —

The Prophet SAW once stood for qiyaam reciting one ayah over and over again. (Surah Al-Maidah, 5:118)

A lot of the companions were known to do this actually - just stand in prayer reciting one ayah over and over again. Many times crying while doing this.

"But if you can stand up and reflect on one ayah - it is better than reading a thousand ayahs with no contemplation" – Sh. Omar Suleiman

Each ayah of the Quran is important and you can write dissertations on just one ayah. So why not stand and contemplate on it - on how it sounds, on what it means, on what Allah is conveying, on what it means in relation to your life at this moment.

Many of you may have a favorite ayah that you know in it's English translation. But you may not know the Arabic of it. It's easy to pull out ayahs - just google something like Quran and *blank*. It's the same way people find quotes to put on their instagram captions. It's another thing to actually fall in love with an ayah.

And you all know what the popular favorite ayahs are. "Verily with hardship there is ease" is perhaps the most common ayah referenced during hard times. But listen to it in Arabic, memorize it in Arabic - I promise you it is even more beautiful in Arabic than it is in English. (Surah Al-Inshirah, 94:5)

So I implore you - whether you have the time or not (and you have the time, don't play games on your phone or search for music, spend like one train ride with the ayah and you'll have it memorized) - find the ayah first. The one that helps you - the one that you love - a happy one or a sad one or an empowering one or a scary one - they are all there.

Memorize the Arabic - listen to it with different reciters, discover that you might even be able to memorize the surah it is in because it might be a short surah. Think about YOUR life.

Don't keep these ayahs as abstract things. The Quran wasn't sent to be abstract. It was sent to heal YOU. It was sent for YOU. Allah is talking to YOU.

— — —

So I reviewed all the surahs I know (it's not a lot), including the ones in the last juz, that we learned when we were kids. Here's what I found:

1) I need to strengthen the ending of the big surahs. I know the first page and second page and then by the third page it's all jumbled up; I start stuttering and confusing ayahs with other surahs. My friend said it's because we review the beginnings as we are memorizing the ending so the beginning becomes super strong without us really

trying. But the ending we only do up until we memorize it and then we move on to another surah. And then I realized how true that is. Even when reviewing surahs in salaah, we tend to recite the beginning and we get to a good midpoint and end it there. This is why the ending is completely lost if we don't review.

2) I have mistakes. In surahs that I think I know hands down, I still have mistakes. I change 'ayns into alifs, I sometimes end ayahs with the noon sound instead of meem. That's a huge deal. That changes the entire sentence. It changes the entire word. It changes the entire meaning of the ayah itself. Not only is that bad - it has the potential to be blasphemous really easily.

3) I can't recite my childhood surahs slowly. Like if I try, I forget the next ayah. I have to do it super fast - all in one go. And that's bad because we are supposed to recite and reflect. I'm speeding through ayahs that are so heavy - about fires and destruction and the Day of Judgment and people Allah is angry at. For example - so many of you guys know Surah Lahab - the last two ayahs mean: His wife shall carry the (crackling) wood - As fuel!- A twisted rope of palm-leaf fibre round her (own) neck! -- WHOA. Right?

For those of us who don't know Arabic - we just sing song the ayahs. Oh how pretty the rhyme. Or how quickly it flows from our tongues.

But that wasn't the purpose of you memorizing them.

Reflection, not just recitation.

A friend of mine said "You don't need to be a hafidh. You are a hafidh of the amount of Quran you have memorized." - Meaning, you need to protect that which you do have memorized - fix it, beautify, correct it. And you need to live by the Quran you have memorized. That would require knowing what it really means. And that would change everything about our prayers and what we recite.

This shouldn't deter you from memorizing. Because - tell me. What other lines could you memorize that would raise your rank in Jannah? What other book will give you robes that cascade down and crowns of light for your parents.

And if it's hard - try harder. Use all your resources - try transliteration if the Arabic is too difficult. And remember that the Quran was orally transmitted and therefore - if you wanted, you could potentially learn it simply by listening over and over and over again. Start - even if you learn one surah a year. It's one more than last year? It's one more surah you get to use in salaah. It's one more chapter of the Quran that can intercede for you!

"The likeness of the one who reads Quran and memorizes it is that he is with the righteous honourable scribes. The likeness of the one who reads it and tries hard to memorize it even though it is difficult for him, he will have two rewards." [Bukhari]

& if you want a surah to start with - Inshirah? Duha? Mulk? Jumu'ah?

— — —

"Do not scatter the (recitation of) Qur'an out like the scattering of sand, and do not rush through it like the hasty recitation of poetry. Stop at its amazing parts and make your heart move with it. None of you should let his concern be to reach the end of the chapter." — Ibn Mas'ood

It is not about a finish line. It is about your journey, your connection, your implementing of what Allah is conveying to you. It's about finding an ayah so powerful to yourself that you have to stop and pray two rakats because you need to bow to the greatness of your Master.

It's like a love letter. Absorb every sentence. Beautify each syllable. Color your world with His magnificence.

Skies might be on lockdown. Angels spreading their wings around every gathering. Angels sitting with you in the emptiness of your room. Everyone seeking one thing only. The pleasure of Allah.

— — —

"As your love for the Quran grows, I won't have to convince you to give it ten minutes out of your day. You will sit with it for more than that. It will happen on its own." - Ustaadh Nouman Ali Khan

For many Muslims, the Quran is a book you open during Ramadan. That's literally it. It's pretty and it just sits there and collects dust.

For some it's a book that they open once in a blue moon as well. Like when they feel sad. Or a hardship touches them.

(By book I mean the physical mushaf - because nowadays "perceived religiousity" is becoming a fad and we have people attaching Quran ayahs to all their Instagram posts and Facebook statuses with no idea about the original arabic ayah or the tafseer of that ayah.)

For others it's a book for weekends, perhaps Sunday school and review. And then there are those who literally designate time during every single day to sit with it alone.

For some of us - praying is enough worship and takes up so much time when we have school work and work and family obligations. But people do designate an hour or two or three even amongst their incredibly busy lives, just to sit with the words of the one who created the sea and the sun.

Everyone has the Quran on their phone. That's easy. But it's a complete different experience from reciting from the mushaf itself.

And it's different from reciting out loud.

Carry the mushaf. It does a few different things:

1) It forces you to have wudhu at all times. So you're constantly at a pure physical state.

2) It serves as a physical reminder. You have the words of Allah with you. Although we all know that Allah is constantly watching us - having his words so close to us physically creates this bubble. This bubble where there isn't gossiping or swearing or watching inappropriate things. It forces you to be aware of your surroundings. You won't be looking at a music video or a billboard when you have the Quran right next to you.

3) If you're carrying it, you'll feel guilty to take out your phone and mindlessly scroll - because you have something far more important with you.

"The Quran is not a free treasure. You have to be worthy of it. You have to put in time." – Ustaadh Nouman Ali Khan

———

"We will be answering Allah - how we sat on this treasure and we couldn't make time for it. But there's plenty of time for TV and friends." – Ustaadh Nouman Ali Khan | Gems from Surah Waqiah

Just how often do you pick up the Quran. And not just have it on your phone but actually interact with it.

Some of your friends are finishing the Quran every month. Month after month. And you have no idea. Some of them are memorizing Surahs every week and you have no idea. Some are reviewing a juz a day and you don't know.

You can't fathom spending time to do these things after working and schoolwork and midterms. Where do they have the time? Do they not study? Do they not sleep? Do they not socialize?

But you've cuddled in your bed with Netflix. You've spent time with your friends when you have midterms and finals.

But to pick up the mushaf, that's too much.

The Quran you rush to finish during Ramadan is the same one sitting on your shelf.

Don't degrade the words of Allah into strips of words you post on social media. It's not your encyclopedia of quotes.

The TV shows and the friends won't be laying in your grave with you. They won't help you answer the questions you'll be asked, 6 feet under the earth.

———

"There are stories about the disbelievers sneaking around to hear the Quran because they knew it was unique, they knew it crossed all bounds of poetry, they knew the Prophet was illiterate. So they tried character assassination to convince people that the messenger was not credible so people would shut him off before even hearing the Quran. Because they knew there was no way to refute the Quran." -- [Paraphrased from Sh. Omar Suleiman's Tafseer of Surah Qalam; Hard Earned]

It's actually so sad how little time we give this book compared to our other books. Our textbooks, our facebooks, our harry potter books. We have all the time in the world for other things except the Quran.

People literally died to spread the message that this book carries. The Prophet was abused, slandered, his heart was shattered, and all he had to offer was this book. He wasn't rich, he didn't heal people, all he had was this book.

That lays somewhere in your room. That you open during Ramadan. Or during a hardship. Or once a week - if that.

That you read without understanding. With no idea when a verse was revealed and the impact of it to the people of that time. The nature of the verse and it's correlation to others.

So tell Him, what was the point of this life if you couldn't give Him a few minutes. If you couldn't hear His words. If you were so busy with the blessings He gave you but completely forgot His letter to you. You want to get close to Him but you want the easy way.

Except Jannah isn't free. And this book is no ordinary book. The first word of this religion was 'Iqraa'. So read before you're given a book on your left hand.

——— ——— ———

"The Qurʿān was meant to be acted upon, but people took reciting it as the required deed." - Hasan Al Basri

It is not enough that we recite it. Just as the hafidh isn't guaranteed Jannah unless they acted upon it - we too are held responsible for acting upon it.

Firstly - have you ever read the entire thing in English? Do you even know the definitions of half the Surahs you have memorized?

The Quran was sent as a guidance - how can it guide you in a language you don't understand? How can it guide you if you only depend on other people to relay its teachings to you. How can it guide you if you only open it during Ramadan.

Don't get me wrong - the recitation of Quran, or even listening to

Quran, is a form of worship. But, it's so much better worshiping a God you love, a God you understand, a God you admire. And it's so amazing to kind of know what you're listening to or reading - to know where it comes from, when it was revealed, what stories lurked behind its revelation, what incidents happened, how the ayahs were used to motivate people, to give people strength.

So find that time, make that time, even if it's 5 minutes a week - study for your akhira while you study for the dunya.

— — —

"Nothing should affect the heart more than the Quran - no lecture, no music, no nasheed, no youtube clip - nothing is greater than the words of Allah." - Sh. Omar Suleiman

So even if you think music helps you study - it doesn't. It's Allah who helps you study. It's Allah who gave you your intellect. He created mankind "ahsani taqweem" the best stature, an excellent moulding.

And no speaker should make you burst into tears the way the Allah's words are supposed to. No nasheed should melt your heart the way Quran should.

Even when you don't know Arabic, you can feel the effect of the words in your heart.

& if you can't feel it - start by cleaning out the specks of darkness - and then listen to the tafseer of Surah Naba. And you'll cry in the middle - you'll find ayahs that'll make you shake in fear, and ayahs that'll make you swell with hope.

— — —

"Islam's interpretative tradition exists because the differences between plain and hidden, elliptical and direct, absolute and qualified, are not always obvious." - Caner K. Dagli

And this is why studying tafseer is so important. More so than just reading the translation of the book in English. You're missing out on so much more - the brilliance of each word, the stories hidden behind the revelation of that particular ayah, the beautiful nuances of the grammar itself.

There is a world of things you don't know about the surahs you monotonously whisper in prayer. And you wonder when you'll ever get khushoo' in prayer. You wonder why you don't feel that thing people talk about. You wonder why you can't enjoy praying like the sahabas did.

Imagine an arrow wounding you while you're in prayer but you just take out the arrow and continue reciting, and then another arrow comes, and you just keep taking them out of your wounded body and keep reciting because you love reciting the words of Allah and "death would have been dearer to me than that the recitation of this surah should be interrupted" - and we hear a text message beep and decide three ayahs are good enough.

Except you don't have the time to study tafseer. But you do have the time to scroll mindlessly through facebook, instagram, tumblr, snapchat, switching back and forth between these apps, waiting for something new.

You have the time to rewatch all your favorite shows on netflix, and to sit on youtube clicking through video after video of hijab tutorials you'll never use, makeup tutorials you don't need, compilation of vines that aren't even that funny, cooking videos you'll never try, and workout videos as you lay in bed for hours.

And one day all of this will be obsolete. One day, it will no longer be worthwhile. One day there will be an angel crossing off your name from their list. And that day will come with no notifications. And it might be too late to make prayers perfect, to fall in love with the Quran, to change unproductive habits.

— — —

"The one who created death and life. This organizes Muslim consciousness. The first thing for us is not life. The first thing is death. That's the initial state. And we are brought out of death into life. First the body of Adam AS is created, this dead corpse, soil, that's all it is. And then life is blown into it. Death was made first. [...] life itself is an additional gift." - paraphrased from Tafseer of Surah Mulk by Ustaadh Nouman Ali Khan

See, every single chapter of the Quran is jaw-dropping beautiful. Not just in the way it sounds and the way it feels to recite them. But also in the linguistic and grammatical intricacies, the back stories of the verses, the connections to other verses and surahs.

But how would you know if you're knee deep in your textbooks, and eyes glued to Netflix.

The access we have to information right now is incomparable - this access comes with a catch - you will be asked how you spent your time.

Are you going to stammer that you did do all your five daily prayers and that was good enough? Like, Allah, I wasn't bad, I prayed all five, on time and everything. And I went to Jummah!

So what about His book? Was that not as important as your relaxation time? As your socializing time? As your tv time?

Youtube is still free. Ilmflix is free. Libraries are free. It's you who decides what to do with your free time.

So pick a surah and fall in love.

— — —

The Quran is supposed to MAKE YOU CRY.

It is the WORDS of Allah. How do I even get this across through text. The gravity of these words. Divine? Does that even explain it?

How does your heart not shake when you hear ayahs about the devastation that will happen. When you hear ayahs about how angry Allah will be at those who disobeyed. The ayahs about the severity of the Day of Judgement and all that is inside Hell.

How does your heart not melt when you hear ayahs on His unlimited forgiveness. How He knows every secret in your heart. How He promises you relief.

How can you allow yourself to be desensitized to the words of Allah?

Stand up after isha with the lights off. Sob. Two rakats of prayer. Cry in the first rakat. Cry so much that you can't even vocalize the ayahs as you are standing. Fall into prostration and cry when you're closest to Him. Beg Him. Beg Him to give you peace and ease and comfort.

Beg Him to heal you.

Stop crying into pillows and cry into your prayer rug instead.

Cry to the Creator who enabled you to have emotions, who enabled you to express emotions, who enabled the cells and organs in your body to function so that you ARE able to cry.

And if you can't cry to Quran - you better play some heavy Quran, stop the music for a week at least - read the actual meanings of the ayahs as they are playing. Sit on your bed, stare at the youtube clip, wait, wait until the dark spots of your heart clear off and you can finally cry again.

Check your imaan. Can you cry because of the Quran?

——— ——— ———

It's beautiful that Allah takes the words right out of our mouth.

Like He knows exactly what we want to say to Him. So much better than we ourselves know; so His wording in His book somehow encompasses everything we want to say to Him.

Except, even more beautifully so. More eloquently so.

Articulated with the utmost precision; perfection from the source of all good, the Perfect One.

So whatever it is you're feeling. Whatever it is you need. I'm sure you could find it in the crevices of your mushaf.

"Do not hold us accountable if we forget or make a mistake. [Surah Al-Baqarah]

"Do not make us bear a burden for which we have no strength." [Surah Al-Baqarah]

"Pour out on us patience." [Surah Al-A'raf]

"Grant us from Yourself mercy and prepare for us from our affair right guidance." [Surah Al-Kahf]

And there are so many secrets in this book. But secrets are for friends. And the deepest secrets are reserved for best friends.

And they really come out in the last third of the night. After a blanket of quiet.

So when will the Quran spill its secrets to you?

— — —

"Imagine a person has some bread in their bag. And someone else has flour in their bag. If the first person got hungry, they could take out the bread and eat it. But the second person would need assistance. They would need a kitchen and eggs and other things to make that flour into bread to eat. So imagine someone has the entire Quran, and you only have bits and pieces of it. When they are told to recite and rise in rank in Jannah, you would have to attempt to make due with the small amount you have, the flour that needs help." - Sheikh Wael Rezk

If you truly loved your Lord, you wouldn't say you have time to kill, and you would never use the term 'bored' because you would always have something to do.

You have a solid hour on the train sometimes, and you simply play music and let your mind wander.

Do you think the Angels next to you with pens, writing down your deeds, do you think they are happy?

What could they have been writing in that hour and what did they write instead?

They could have wrote "so-and-so glorified Allah, made Dua, memorized a line of Quran" but instead it's "so-and-so is listening to music".

Can't you just feel the Angels sighing whenever you do something silly. It might not be haram things but it's just wasted time. Time you could be using to fill up books and books, stacking good deeds just by reading a line. In arabic. In transliteration. In translation. However way you wish. It's the words of your Lord.

And for those who have memorized parts, strengthen them. Why lose the gift Allah blessed you with? Especially if you memorized so much at a young age. Do you have any idea how jealous people are of you?

Even if you just have juzz amma down - that's more Quran than half the population of Muslims have!

& for those who have memorized the whole thing, know that you're blessed with a gift and no one has more of an obligation to teach it than you. Teaching does not mean going to a masjid and teaching children. It can mean your sibling. It can mean your best friend.

It should not be weird to see people in the library studying Quran the way they study for finals.

Cause this is more important than a final exam. This is about your final destination. This is the exam.

by Time,
mankind
is in loss

"[To the young people] You don't have something called free time, guys. You don't. You are members of this ummah. Every member of this ummah is constantly working to make this society better. To do something good for people. You don't time to play video games for 8 hours, you don't have time for the new movie that's coming out, you have time to do more important things. Hold yourself to a higher standard." - Ustaadh Nouman Ali Khan

We have to be amazing students, amazing members in our individual fields - don't just be a premed student - be THE premed student, don't just have whatever grades, get THE grades. And then also - seek Islamic Knowledge, seminars and lectures, books and Quran. And then also spend time with family and friends.

With all of these things to do - how can you possibly have free time to waste away - don't get me wrong, Allah said we can enjoy - we can enjoy a movie with our friends, we can have some relaxing down time with a few episodes of a show. But are we really that free that we can watch countless hours of TV? With the Quran just sitting there. With a pool of information we're supposed to seek and know.

Just because it's summer vacation - doesn't mean we get completely lazy and watch tv all day. And DON'T wait for Ramadan to get on an imaan high! And we say we're too busy to do this and that during the school year, well when school is over, what's our excuse?

As we grow older, the excuses will pile up - we have family to feed, we have bills to pay, work to do, events to attend, children to take care of - remember - take advantage of your youth. This is the time.

— — —

"Live life in such a way that when you die, you are dearly missed." Mufti Ismail Menk

What kind of mark will you leave behind in this Dunya? Will it be positive or negative? These are questions we should be asking everyday to ourselves. If the average lifespan is 60-70 years of age, then our lives are relatively short. Ask an elderly person, they'll will tell you that their lives flashed right by. We need to constantly use our time wisely.

It's true, Allah told us that mankind is already in loss off time. It goes by SO fast. Think about it in terms of school, oh those middle school days, high school days, college?

You can never get the same time back. You will never get back this day, this minute. Are you using it wisely?

The Prophet did SO much. Forget the fact that almost half his life he didn't actually have Islam. And then he fights all these battles. He also has to solve like every families family drama. But then again - he also played games with his wives. And everyone who met him thought he was their best friend. How did he manage to do that? He took care of his community, his best friends, his acquaintances, even the friends of his wives were welcomed into his home and he was always consciously making an effort to make people happy.

Live life in such a way that you strive to be the best, best in your worship, in your academic/career life, among your community members. You can't please everyone - but please Allah, and He will put love in people's heart for you too. And be happy.

— — —

"You have to water this relationship with Allah all the time." - Sh. Hatem Al Haj

You know, people think "religious" people got it all. They must be at peace all the time. They have so many good deeds, and they pray all their prayers on time, and they must get all their duas answered.

That's not the case. If you speak to these "religious" people, the more practicing friends of yours - they've been through insanity. It didn't happen overnight. And it still takes a lot from them. They still have inner battles, they still struggle with having patience and tawakkul. They still have to work hard to get rewarded by Allah.

There's a reason why the Prophet's most frequent dua was: "O Turner of the hearts, make my heart firm upon Your Religion."

It takes a lot to find contentment. It's fighting shaytaan every morning, and fighting your own nafs every second.

It is not easy to battle your own self.

It is not easy to get out of bed to physically pray and recite Quran.

It is not easy to "find time" for the deen when you have other priorities in life from school and work to family and self care.

It takes effort. A hafidh doesn't have it made. They aren't done with the Quran. They review. A scholar doesn't finish after they get their diploma. They are constantly reading, rereading, reteaching, re-memorizing. No one is done. No one has it all figured out. No one found the zenith of ibadah.

And when you have deen, it can go away. When hardships and battles and doubts are pushed onto you - you can fall off your deen.

One day you can be the person who does qiyaam, and the next day you can be the person who doesn't pray.

You have to put in the effort. You have to want His love every day and do things to deserve it.

And love is shown through actions. So how did you profess your love to Him today?

— — —

I used to think that I could easily answer the questions you get asked in the grave.

Who is your Lord? Allah. Of course.

But if you didn't live your life praising Allah, obeying Allah, glorifying Allah, remembering Allah, thanking Allah. Your tongue might get tied. Your memory might go blank - like it does after you've memorized the flashcard a million times, but somehow on the exam, all you see is a white index card.

Who is your Lord?

To whom did you worship when you speeded through your prayers? To whom did you worship when you aced your exams and didn't thank Him, rather felt like you did it all. To whom did you worship when you found sorrow and chose entertainment over His Quran.

The heaviness of "la ilaha ilallah". It's not just believing. Its all encompassing. With that belief comes the rules, the obedience, the understandings, the trust that He knows everything.

And then the question - Who is your Prophet?

You only know his name. And that he prayed more than you ever did. And that he sacrificed a lot. But the wars he fought and the treaties he made are jumbled somewhere in your mind. The seerah, the biography so few of us read, so few of us know inside out. The actions he told us to stay away from - you didn't stay away. The softness in his character, you didn't emulate. The nonjudgmental demeanor, you didn't echo.

And what is your religion?

But did we practice and study and learn and understand enough of the religion to answer.

Because these are the questions. The ones that have no cheat sheet. The ones you cannot memorize and regurgitate. The ones you cannot answer simply by "knowing".

— — —

"This world is nothing but a number of days." – Boonaa Mohammed

Short and simple, real talk time.

If you've got time for a Netflix binge, you've got time for the extra two rakats of sunnah, and yeah, a little nafl won't hurt.

If you've got cash for a starbucks venti, you've got cash for the homeless person.

If you're willing to do all-nighters for exams, you should be even more willing to do all-nighters for the biggest test of your life, to get into Jannah, not med school, not law school, but Jannah.

And if you've got time to kill with friends, you have time to find out your parents favorite things and make more than just small talk with your family.

If your life is a number of days. Well, let's do the math. Average person lives about 82 years. Most of you are in your 20s let's say, so you have about 60 years left. If calculated in months, you have 720 months left. In days, it's about 21,900 days left. Plus or minus the time you spend sleeping and doing the necessary worldly things like earning an income or spending time with loved ones - what percentage of it is really going towards worship, and what percentage is towards wasteful things.

Let every day be a new chance to show Allah how madly you love Him.

— — —

"So tell me, what do you love? The adornments of this world – or the one they come from?" - Boona Mohammed

Sometimes we get preoccupied with these adornments. The books, the jewelry, the clothes, the phones, the Netflix.

But this world is nothing but a big distraction. What is your time spent on most? What is your heart attached to? What is your addiction?

Is it to worship Him the way He deserves to be worshipped, or to waste more time in this big distracting world?

— — —

In the tafseer of Surah Ar-Rahman it is mentioned that the sequence of the ayahs is somewhat strange.

"We would expect the sequence to be Allah saying that He created the human being and then taught the Qur'an. What kind of sequence is this? There are two things: existence and purpose of existence. As far as Allah is concerned, your purpose is even more important than your existence. The reason for which you were created is more important than your creation itself. Allah mentions the document that makes sure you have your purpose and then our existence. Allah mentions the purpose first." - Ustaadh Nouman Ali Khan

People wonder their entire life - "what is the purpose of life?" People with the highest of status and all of the fame and glory and drugs and sex - all of the people who are turnt up every night - all of them still seek to find purpose at one point or another. Some continue to fulfill carnal desires and go down a bad path. Others use that desire for purpose and channel it into charity work.

Your Lord already gave you your purpose. To busy your life in worship of Him.

This doesn't mean to tire yourself out by just praying salah all day. It means to remember Him in every aspect of your life. Every minute of your life. It means to let the intention of everything go back to Him.

Study to get a career that can help people because through this you are seeking His pleasure. Study to please your parents with good grades because pleasing them is an act of worship. Work to feed your family is an act of worship. Going out with your friends to cheer someone up is an act of worship. Playing basketball to stay fit and take care of your body is an act of worship. All of it is an act of worship if and only if you want it to be. If your intention is pure, then the act is written as your good deed.

It's not hard - to worship your Creator. It is harder to disobey. Because disobeying means going against your own fitrah, it means silencing the moral compass in your mind, it means swallowing the feelings of guilt after sinning until you no longer get those feelings, it means disappointing your parents.

Allah made this religion easy so don't make it hard on yourself. And if you still don't understand the purpose, the instruction manual is right there, perhaps in a cupboard getting dusty or atop a shelf in the living room. Pick it up.

— — —

"When you want to succeed as bad as you wanna breathe than you will be successful." - Eric Thomas

Listen to the adhan - what does it say? "Hasten to success"

What does Allah say about the believers? "They are on (true) guidance from their Lord, and they are the successful." (Surah Al-Baqarah)

Everywhere, in every aspect of your life, your goal should be succeed.

If you want something - Jannah, a career, a righteous loving family, a fit body, academic excellence, anything - you HAVE to work for it.

Yeah, right, how cliche is this? Here's the thing - cliches exist for a reason. Now is it as simple as saying work for it? Of course you want to work for it. But you might need some practical steps:

Wake up early - The Prophet said Allah placed a special blessing in the time after Fajr until Noon. Try it out. Even if you're not a morning person - TRY IT. There are countless books and studies that explain why waking up early helps you be productive. Gosh, I think about all those days I would wake up at noon or after even, it literally kills the day, like you just wasted half an entire day!

Put the TV Off - (or anywhere you're watching movies or shows) Realize that it eats away your time, seconds, minutes, hours go by that you could have spent doing something more productive and even more fun!

To-Do-Lists - Try them too. And write outrageous stuff if you want to, or even far off goals.

You have SO much potential. You have a ton inside you. A brain Allah gave you. A body Allah molded with perfection. Make Him happy, make your parents happy, make your future children happy.

Allah didn't put us on this earth to just go by, to be mediocre. YOU are NOT mediocre. You were chosen by Him.

So go do the crazy goal you never thought you could do - go memorize the Quran, go on and wear hijab, go on and get a 2400 on the SATs, go get that 4.0 or summa cum laude diploma, go get that dream job, you're in charge of your future. Make it happen.

— — —

You know how often times it feels like the Quran is talking to other people. Like it's telling polytheists that they should look at the signs of the Oneness of Allah.

And it's almost like, but I know you, Allah. I already affirm to your oneness and your majesty and your greatness.

So why should we read those ayahs? And why are they everywhere?

Because sometimes we become like the polytheists. Let me explain:

Contemplating on the ayah from Surah Tur: Or do they have a God other than Allah?

Well we don't. But then ... we give into our nafs - our own body, our self. So if we're tired, we will use the shortest surahs to pray just to get to bed sooner. Or if we're hungry, we might go overboard gluttonous and then even end up wasting food.

Or we give importance to things over our worship. Like we would rather watch tv all night instead of praying just a few extra nawafil. Or school studies over Quran studies.

And it's hard to find a balance sometimes. But we should at least be trying?

If we keep God in perspective - and not just as a supreme being that answers our dunya duas - then we won't give into societal pressures, our own badness - plus, we would find peace. Actually peace. Tranquility-peace. Like that peace when you wake up on a summer morning without an alarm because you literally have nothing to do. This organic kind of peace.

So the ayahs - they're to remind, constantly, to realign our day, to realign our life, our worries, and put everything into perspective.

What have you replaced in your life as God? Yourself? Your academic goals? Money? Entertainment? Fitness? Friends? -- None of these things are inherently evil, but each one has a due right upon you - and each one should also align with your ultimate goal: pleasing Allah, the One, the Only, the Forever.

— — —

"In the pursuit of excellence, you cannot be looking below you. [...] You consistently have to look above and think: what more can I do to please Allah, what more can I do to accomplish great things?" - Sh. Omar Suleiman

We pat ourselves in the back for praying five times, for praying thahajjud, for reading Quran, for doing some adhkhar.

But look around you at the people above - be it intangible people like Maryam AS or Umar RA, or even amongst your own friend circles, your own family members, or the facebook stories of the piety of people around the world.

You are barely touching the surface. And it's not impossible. If Allah got you this close - He can get you closer.

To a non muslim - praying 5 times sounds ridiculous. Five whole times a day? Like, you stop and you have to pray? Every day?

To you - it's normal. You can't imagine life without it really.

But then to others - the valedictorians of Jannah - to them it's bare minimum and incomplete without the added sunnahs and nawafil and long standing and long sujoods.

Even apart from worship - don't look below you in academics or your own goals. Don't say "well at least I'm not failing". If you want to be excellent go for the A, not the A-.

If you want to be mediocre, in your worship and in your dunya goals, then know that you're doing an injustice to yourself.

"Read your record. Sufficient is yourself against you this Day as accountant." (Surah Al-Isra)

— — —

"Nothing about your body impresses Allah. Not your citizenship. Not your wealth. Not your looks. Not your status. He looks at your spiritual makeup." - Sheikh Hamza Maqbul

The thing about wealth and status and looks - who gives it to you? Allah. So why would He be pleased with any of it?

All of that is the dunya. It's for you.

Yes, wealth can help you donate more, status can help you have more of a voice in important matters - all of this is important.

But when you start chipping away your spiritual makeup for these things - that's when you're in trouble.

So if your education is "in the way" of you praying on time: you need to fix your priorities. Or if your homework is making you quicken your worship, that's a problem too.

If your status is making you forget your family in need, if your status is making you judge and look down at others, something is not right.

If your busy life is preventing you from reading Quran, that's a problem.

Cause doing good deeds is great, but it's greater if it's combined with a beautiful spiritual relationship with Allah. Or maybe those deeds will be blown away by the wind right before you face Allah. Right before He asks you about your salaah: is it complete or is it lacking?

— — —

"The messengers of Allah are being told not to be lazy in dhikr. And we think we do enough dhikr." – Ustaadh Nouman Ali Khan

When we were small we used to feel good about going to bed at night after saying Surah Al-ikhlaas three times and the dua before sleeping. Some of us have long forgotten about that. We sleep after our fingers get tired of clicking between snapchat, instagram and facebook. After our eyes can't look at the bright phone screen any longer.

We feel accomplished doing the tasbeeh after our five daily prayers - if we even do that - if we aren't zooming through and going onto the next task on our day.

On trains and busses we think of ways to pass our time - music, videos, games, daydreaming.

A couple of duas a day and we feel like we covered it. The morning dhikr, the leaving house dua, saying bismillah before eating. We did what Allah asks of us.

But every time you say you're bored, it's like an angel rolling their eyes because goodness gracious - your death is so close by, what do you mean you're bored. What if those five extra minutes of dhikr, literally just remembering the greatness of Allah, is what tips the scale on your favor.

It's like you have a bank account and you need a certain amount to get into Jannah. Everytime you say "subhanAllah" and like mean it - like whoa look at that moon, look at that rain, look at that people, look at that flawless perfection, listen to that wind - you're adding cash to your account.

And then for every swear, every second of gossip, every ughh to your mother, every late prayer, every hastened prayer, your cash levels go down. For all we know - it could be a balance of negative - EVEN if we are praying five times and covering basics.

So make it positive - the smallest of things can bring the biggest of rewards. You want Jannah - but you can't give an extra five minutes?

Is dhikr so hard that you can sit watching a 45 minute show, but glorifying Allah a few times feels tiring.

Is our Lord not giving enough that we should be thankful - just with our tongue - not even with our limbs.

— — —

"Oh man, what made you so careless concerning your Lord, the Most Generous?" - Surah Infitar, 82:6

When we are about to send in a paper to be published (not your procrastinated in two-hour term paper), we edit like a paranoid perfectionist.

When we get ready for important guests, we clean so it's impeccable.

When we are about to take big exams like the MCAT, LSAT, GMAT, we study as if our whole life depended on this one thing.

When we get dressed for an event, we meticulously take our time to make things flawless, creaseless.

But when we pray, we quicken it. We let our mind wander. We pray at the last minute. We slump into rukoo', and passively whisper in sujood. We use surahs we use in every prayer - repetitively, monotonously, lazily, without comprehension.

When we read Quran (if we do regularly), we carelessly read, zooming through parts we know, with no reflection what so ever. But this book has the power to make mountains into dust. "If We had sent down this Qur'an upon a mountain, you would have seen it humbled and coming apart from fear of Allah." (Surah Al-Hashr, 59:21)

We do our physics homework with accuracy, we double check our answers during exams, we reread emails and texts before sending them - but to our Lord we stand in a lethargic, lackadaisical manner. To our Lord, we speed through Surah Al-Ikhlaas.

But these are the things that actually matter. In the end - you won't have your 4.0, your SAT scores, your career, your beautiful spouse, your best friends. All you'll have are deeds; points in a book handed to you on your right hand, or your left hand as you attempt to hide it behind your back. What is in the book?

— — —

"Your dream doesn't have an expiration date. Take a deep breath and try again."

Let's focus on the dream of entering Jannah.

We mess up, and we keep messing up. Even the people you might deem as "religious" also sin. We don't know what they do in the depths of the night. We don't know how they are with their families. We don't know their tongue outside of their speeches at events.

We build people up and feel that we will never get to Jannah when Allah has people who worship Him the way these "religious" people do.

Except you could be there. You could be with Allah Himself, at the highest level of Jannah, talking to Him and Him actually responding to you.

There is an expiration date: your death.

But every minute is a minute to start over. Even if you just finished sinning - you just finished watching something haraam, or smoking, drinking, backbiting, cursing, or feeling holier-than-thou - you get to turn around and say - nope. No. I'm not doing this again. I want Allah's pleasure, not the momentary pleasure of my nafs and not the pleasure of the people around me.

If you haven't prayed, pray now. If you haven't read Quran in ages, read it now. If you're feeling dead inside, just go to sujood. Keep pressing refresh - it's a start over button, again and again and again.

So we try. We fail. We get back up. We cry again to Him.

Even when the Earth slips from underneath you, it's Allah that keeps you firm. Keep going, refresh, beam at the sky.

"Even champions need to practice."

So practice longer, practice harder.

— — —

"Just when you are done, when you figure that you are burnt out - you're really not. You'll realize you had more to give. You'll regret it if you don't." - Noelle Hickey

You can always do more. When you were younger, you thought a few hours of homework was your breaking point. But after SAT classes and college and med school and grad school, you realize those hours weren't the breaking point. There are kids who did way more than you. There are kids who went to school with amazing grades, also studied hifz, also learned a sport or did karate or had a talent they cultivated (or were forced to do so by parents) and also went to tutoring. Maybe you were that kid.

But wherever you are now - this is not your breaking point. For those of you in just school - you're having a hard time balancing schoolwork and extracurricular activities and social life and seeking Islamic knowledge. You have it easy. It only gets harder. Anyone who is older will tell you how much harder it gets. When you have so much more to worry about like paying bills and installments and taxes and still keeping Quran in your daily routine while balancing work and family and all while making sure there are eggs and milk in the fridge.

Life isn't meant for it to be a free ride. And you are capable of more than you give yourself to be.

You ever met those people who seem to have it all? The dunya and the akhira tied together. The ones who have stellar academic grades, are social butterflies loved by everyone, probably have the Quran memorized, amazing manners, and still somehow pray qiyaam and attend all the cool MSA events.

Sh. Mohamed Faqih mentioned a similar sentiment. "You make it look easy. No, it is easy. Because Allah makes it easy."

It's really about your priorities. If your priority is learning the Quran - it'll take precedence. If it's academics - then that'll be most important. If it's just about having fun and enjoying the moment then that will take up the most time.

Figure out your priorities and divide your daily routine by that.

Prayer should be the first thing you fix. And then be realistic. Will you read a page of Quran a day? Can you keep that up? If not - maybe you can read just one line a day? Or maybe you can just listen to it? Can you get As? (I think every single person is capable of getting a 4.0 - it's about what you put in + Allah's help) How many volunteer hours do you need? Are you adding enough knowledge of the deen into your life regularly?

Also. Successful people snip away the unnecessary time fillers.

Successful people don't watch tv.

Studies show that 67% of successful, rich people, watch less than an hour of TV a day.

So go get your success for both worlds. If you think you're on the right track for the akhira then also step up your game and be successful in the dunya, be a role model for the future. And if you've got dunya in your belt then you must shape up your akhira.

"If you fall asleep now, you will dream. If you study now, you will live your dream." - Harvard Motivational Blog.

And Allah won't help you until you help yourself. Go get on those dreams.

— — —

"Rest if you must, but don't you quit." - tumblr

Whatever goal you have in mind - rest if you have to - but do not give up.

If you're memorizing Quran and you're stuck on a surah - rest. Take a breather. Review what you know. Study some tafseer. Listen to it over and over. Watch a few motivating lectures. And a week later, get right back into it.

If you're aiming for the 4.0 and feel like crashing - crash. But only for a day. Treat yourself to the day off, with friends or family or your bed and a disney movie. And then get back into gear. Finish the papers, make the flashcards, work for it, get it, make your parents smile.

If you're attempting to lose weight but aching to give up - stop for a day, eat the slice of pizza, stay in your pajamas. But pick up your sneakers the next day and grab your favorite yogurt.

If you're attempting to pray qiyaam, and it's just one of those nights where you can't - don't. Do some dhikr instead, stay in bed and talk to Allah, or make a list of things you want in Jannah. Take your night off, but the next day - back into the zone, back into reciting, back into standing till your legs hurt, and bowing till you feel like you are a part of the earth itself.

You are the best of creation: take breaks, re-energize, sleep. And wake up like those face wash commercials - smiling, rejuvenated, ready.

"If you can dream it, you can do it." - Walt Disney

— — —

"Time management is a choice. Even if you think you're not good at it you CAN be good at it. It's about making certain choices." - Dr. Farhan Abdul Azeez

You know they say things like Einstein had the same number of hours in a day as you do. The sahabas also had 24 hours in a day.

But how is it that we hear their stories - the way the earned income and took care of their family obligations and chilled with their buddies and did qiyaam.

In a way, time is subjective and objective - notice how sometimes time goes by sooooo slowly - like in a boring lecture. And other times it flies by, like the weekends.

Allah can give you barakah in your time - you'll notice that sometimes you can finish all your homework in two hours, but other times it takes you a good 6 hours. Time is in the hands of Allah, even though we think it's the same 24 hours in a day - it kind of isn't. Some days feel longer, some days feel shorter, some days you are a superhuman who runs errands and cooks and cleans and writes two papers, on other days you are lucky if you read just one assignment.

If Allah loves that you perfect something - why not step up your game. Do the best you can in school, hand things in on time, your teachers have a right over you. Your family also has rights over your time, as do friends, as does your body. And you need to give Allah and your own soul it's due rights.

Time management isn't a fluffy workshop you take and continue procrastinating and being amazed by other people who look like their life is put together perfectly. Time management is reflecting over Surah Al-Asr, and changing who you are entirely.

— — —

"Why are you more concerned with what you're going to do, than what you're doing? Why aren't you paying attention to how you live your life right this very moment? Why are you wasting this moment? Why, indeed, are you wasting your life?" -- Colin Beaven

I'm going to memorize this surah, I'm going to start fasting soon, I'm going to start learning tajweed/arabic, I'm going to give up makeup, I'm going to make Quran a priority, I'm going to pray the sunnah portions . . .

What about today? What about - pause your assignments - give forward something for your akhira - today.

We cannot keep making a bucket list of things we hope to accomplish and not work towards these things. We cannot keep waiting for a winter break and a summer break; we will end up waiting forever, because these breaks are a facade. Your parents don't have these breaks. Once you're out of school, you also won't have these breaks. Once the career, the household, the kids, the family obligations, once those things happen - these breaks no longer exist.

So it may be finals month, it may be applications month - but you have to find a way. Put the dunya on hold for a second and do something, a small something. A line, a verse, a dua, a handful of tasbeeh.

Your life will always feel like it's zooming - you will always be too busy. Just as you're checking things off your to-do list, you will find that it fills up again. So seize a moment - you don't need to carpe diem. Just a millisecond - close your eyes and let the world stop.

& start crossing off things from the more important bucketlist. Things you truly need to get done, because the angel of death doesn't wait for you to finish your degree and become established. The angel of death doesn't wait for your convenience.

— — —

"There's only one thing more precious than our time and that's who we spend it on." - Leo Christopher

But we give pieces to Allah - scrap time - free time - if we find free time - that's when we "squeeze" in a page of Quran, where we fit in the sunnahs or a few nawafil rakats.

One day you will actually read the seerah. One day, you will know all the names of the mothers of the believers. One day you can call Allah by all of His ninety nine names. One day, you'll actually perfect your recitation. One day, you will actually stand a whole night in prayer - okay maybe just a third of the night. One day, you'll read the whole Quran in English. One day, you'll have understood the tafseer of each and every surah. One day, you will do all the things that get you closer to Allah. One day, you'll have time. You just don't have the time now.

But binge watching Netflix - so much so that you've run out of things to watch? No problem. But hanging out with friends for countless hours talking about the same things, you have time for.

Allah is worth more than your "free time".

"The companions had to be reminded to do their part of the dunya, while we have to be reminded to do for the akhira." - Sh. Waleed Basyouni

Why do you have to FIND time for Him - when He is the one who gave you this time in the first place?

the reward
of patience:
immeasurable

"The end goal of shaytaan is to make the people ungrateful." – Sheikh Omar Suleiman

Here's the strange thing - we are always under this assumption that as long as we believe in Allah, we are safe. But the small sins - especially that of ungratefulness to our Lord - are actually a pretty big deal.

Almost all of our small sins can stem from ungratefulness. Cursing - you're ungrateful for the voice and the mouth you were given. Watching haram- you're ungrateful of your eyesight. Disobeying parents, you're ungrateful that your parents are alive and care for you.

And the even smaller things! Our headphones stop working and we get upset. Being ungrateful for an A- when that's really the effort we put in anyway. Being angry when we miss our train. The small seconds of our frustration puts a smile on Shaytaans face because it's a little victory for him. He gets to say - see, they believe in you, but they aren't content, they aren't grateful.

So whenever calamities come. Even our first world problems of slow internet or cold pizza. Say Alhamdulillah. And really believe that Alhamdulillah. Stop your world for a second and praise Him for the calamity. For even those calamities are a blessing.

— — —

"Be mindful of God, and He will take care of you."

This is part of a longer hadith, every line powerful in its own way.

Sometimes we think we control things. But really, we don't control anything at all. And so if we do what He asked of us, and then leave it all up to Him, we will see answers. You have control over nothing, only your own effort.

There really is something about inner peace that makes everything else in the world so meaningless, so simple, so miniscule.

All there is left is you and Allah.

— — —

Iman has two parts: Sabr & Shukr

Over and over again in the Quran, Allah mentions that He is with the patient. But do we really listen to Him? Patience falls into EVERY element of our life.

Patience in justice - when someone wrongs you, you be patient in Allah's decree - even if you don't meet justice here, Allah will make sure you get justice in the hereafter.

Patience with people - whether it be tutoring a small child or teaching someone skills or working in a team or trying to give dawah.

Patience with family - spiritually, culturally, logically, we go through so much family drama, have patience.

Patience with marriage - the right person will come inshaAllah, just have patience.

Patience with grades - you shouldn't say Allah didn't answer your prayer of getting an A in the class. Maybe He has something better planned.

Patience in times of hardship - because there is always light at the end of the tunnel.

Sabr. Patiently waiting for Jannah.

— — —

"When your parents congratulate you - it's one thing. When the dean of the school congratulates you at the inaugural ceremony - it's something else. And when the Prophet (SAW) will congratulate the sabireen (people of patience) and Allah has commanded him to do so ... " – Ustaadh Nouman Ali Khan

Imagine, being congratulated by the prophet himself! Standing in front of the man who loved you before you born and stood in prayer with aching legs just for you - when you yourself don't even want to do the extra few sunnahs.

The sabireen - the patient ones. Patience in the face of adversity. Patience in the face of hardships. From heartbreaks and deaths of loved ones, troubling finances and family drama.

(This isn't referring to cases of patience when abuse is happening! This is speaking in generalities, not exceptions.)

Sabr is beautiful - the pure kind. Not patiently waiting on line to buy something - but real sabr that says Alhamdulillah when the train doors close.

So next time, when the food at the restaurant is just terrible, when the websites choose to take ages to load, when the homework assignment makes absolutely no sense. Remember the ones with patience.

— — —

"First ayah of Surah Fatiha : Rab. Usually translated as "Lord" but it actually comes from "nurture", someone who takes care of you from the beginning of your life till your death." - Mufti Zaid Khan

A Surah we recite several times during the day and we slide through this part, speeding to finish. He is the one taking care of us.

We forget that. All. The. Time. We are so arrogant sometimes without knowing it - we forget that He is actually in charge and we think that WE have control. We have none. Absolute zero control. That's why you can study your butt off for an exam and still fail. That's why you can have the grades to get into Harvard and still get rejected. If Allah doesn't ordain something for you - it will not be yours.

"It is not the degree that gives us sustenance, it is Allah."

Just as Allah provides rain for the plants, and food for the wandering birds. He provides what He wills for you.

So be patient in His provisions - be it in wealth, health, beauty, a spouse, knowledge, and family. If He gives a wandering bird enough food for the day, surely He can find a way to feed a worshiping slave like you.

— — —

"Allah reminds us even in a paper cut that we are not in control" - Sheikh Saad Tasleem

The analogy was that something as harmless as paper can hurt us. And even when we are careful, as we flip pages the paper cut can just happen the second we get careless or sometimes even by accident. And a paper cut is such a small miniscule thing but it can be very bothersome and painful.

We are not in control - of the harm that comes our way, nor the good. So the best we can do is be understanding of the situations we are put in. If harm comes, deal with it, and if it's silly things like gossip or rumors, do away with them, don't lend your ear to them, don't be harmed. Don't give other people the edge that they can harm you because you decide what's harming you. If you're going by the books, trust Him, it'll all be perfect.

And when real harm does come to us, in forms of tests and hardships, we don't control how long we have them or the potential power of that harm. We can only control our perception of it. How do we face it? With grace and patience, or with curses and anger?

What is going to come will come no matter what mountains blocking it, and what isn't meant for you won't come even if you can taste it on your tongue.

— — —

I'm a fairly patient person. But one week, I lost it. It was like one thing after another going wrong. Big things and small things. Big things like scholarship rejections. Small things like I was stuck in a crowded elevator going to the eleventh floor, the elevator decides to stop on the eighth and then come all the way back down and not go to the eleventh and I was stuck on the crowded elevator twice and getting late to class.

Like really - it was the SILLIEST of things after a series of big issues. And I was trying not to let the big issues get to me, but once a string of minuscule things happened - it just broke me apart. I was so upset over so many things that I couldn't even articulate why I was upset.

I was being patient. I kept making dua and being patient. But once I broke, I became out of character. Really for like five hours. I became a different person. It's ridiculous, I know. And I was so frustrated, I was like "That's it. I'm not praying the sunnah for Maghrib today.

Now what."

And it's so silly to think that way. Because really - me not praying doesn't do anything to Allah.

Allah's greatness is still there. People will praise Him regardless. And Allah does not need to be praised by people for Him to be praiseworthy.

Missing a sunnah does nothing to Him. It doesn't even do much for me except that I missed out on some sujood and reward.

And I literally sat on my bed - with no idea what to do with myself. And yes, I know that when people are upset - you listen to Quran, you pray some nafl, it all figures itself out. But I didn't know what I was feeling. Like I had to analyze it all.

It wasn't about feeling better - because I knew I'd feel better eventually. I knew Allah would fix it all eventually. I knew the advice others could give me because I could give it to myself.

But I needed to just say some dumb stuff out loud to someone. So I told my friend to yell at me and argue all my dumb points.

And one of those points was "Why did Allah say He's too shy to return hands empty but then He keeps my hands empty?"

Her response: "Shut up. Your hands aren't empty."

And I kind of stopped.

Yeah, the advice is - remember the blessings you have. Count your blessings. Be grateful. Look at all you have. - But just the way she said it. Just the way it happened.

Sometimes - you need someone to just tell you to shut up.

Sometimes, you don't need advice in a neat package, tied with a feel-good hadith.

Sometimes you know exactly what advice someone would give - you just need to hear it someone else's voice.

Sometimes, you need a slap in the face for being idiotic.

And the great thing is that Allah blessed you with people who would do it - who don't hesitate to set you right, who have the knowledge, who have the words.

And then you go back to Allah humbled. Like curling up to your mom because you feel guilty for not doing something she wanted you to do earlier.

And the beautiful thing is that - that's the point.

The point is to turn back to Him. Even if you didn't really turn away. Even if you became stupid for a few hours. It's because He runs to you when you take a few steps.

Swallow the pride. Realize who you're talking about and who you're talking to. If you don't go back to Him - who are you going to? If He doesn't give - who will?

— — —

"Dua is the weapon of the believer but a weapon is only as powerful as the one who holds it." - Sh. Waleed Basyouni

You all know the power of dua, especially those that get answered instantaneously, and even those that don't get answered the way we liked them to, but a year or so down the line we realize why and it brings a wave of contentment, like subhanAllah, Allah you were right all along.

People are always saying "make dua for me!" all over their social media. Tons of statuses, or tumblr posts, especially during exam times. And a lot of times in passing - in the hall, just someone will say "yeah, inshaAllah, make dua." whether it be about an acceptance into a program, a job interview, a marriage proposal, or a hardship they're facing. And our automatic response is always "of course, inshaAllah, I will keep you in my duas."

But do you? Can you say - 100% - you have made dua for EVERY individual that has asked you to do so? (And no not like "Allah help ˹ll the believers" but like a specific dua, for that specific person).

With social media, these posts go right above our head - the news of a sick person, the graphic videos of children in other countries, the deaths - prayers for so-and-so. The morbid things and the light things.

Maybe we do. Maybe our friends do come to mind when we are in sujood. But acquaintances might not? The exact things they want might not?

But it would literally take a second to make dua. Stop yourself, stop scrolling for just a second, close your eyes and just make the dua. If it's in person, say inshaAllah, but make the dua immediately after, as you're rushing off to class. You have no idea whose duas are accepted and when they're accepted.

Also - we should keep a running list of duas. It's nice to see things getting answered, and we often forget the blessings He bestowed, the things we begged so hard for. A list of duas in a private journal for those random nights where you pray a few extra rakats before bed.

— — —

"Sometimes the 'best choice' isn't always the right choice." – Sheikh Yaser Birjas□

Sometimes the ideal, best college - isn't the college that's right for you. The best career - might not make you happy. The best medical school - might not be your environment. The best program - might break you down physically and mentally.

Sometimes what we think is best for us - isn't always the case.

So it's not about finding the best thing - the perfect spouse, the perfect house, the perfect career. It's about what is right for you - in your life here and in your life for the hereafter. And that comes with reaching for the moon, getting lost in the stars - and understanding that Allah will guide you to your right one, to your right person, to your right path, to your right career.

And that takes a lot of tawakkul. But if we believe Allah can give us Jannah, He guided Yunus out of a whale, He made a way for Maryam to get out of the whispers of people (I mean really - imagine going through labor, by yourself, knowing that when you go back to your people, they will say despicable things, because there is no way we could even explain to someone now, that Allah gave me a child even though I've never been touched by a man - I mean, it's preposterous even now, but she had faith that Allah will make it work out the right way) - so why can't we trust He will give us everything else that's right for us.

"And it may be that you dislike a thing which is good for you and that you like a thing which is bad for you. Allah knows but you do not know." - Surah Al-Baqarah

— — —

I realized how impatient I am with myself and I think it's universal. We forgive our younger siblings for certain things but don't forgive ourselves.

If you get a bad grade, you punish yourself, you hold yourself to a certain standard and then get disappointed if it's not met.

So when you forget to read Quran, you give up the next day too. Or when you waste some time watching something, you end up killing the rest of your day in uselessness too.

You are impatient with your talents, your abilities, your pathway to your accomplishments.

You are impatient with your prayers.

So here's a little perspective:

Shaytaan is perhaps the most patient of all. Relentlessly, coming at people in every direction. With small things. With big things. Someone can be praying on time for years and then one day they don't. Someone might be reading Quran every day and then one day just not. Small addictions that lead people to neglect the important things.

He fails. And then he comes back. He didn't get you to miss one prayer, but he'll get you to be lazy with another. He didn't get you to attend the club but he'll get you see club scenes on tv. You were good for Ramadan and a little after, so he waited a few months before getting you back. You didn't go to that specific party but you'll eventually go to another. Perhaps you didn't curse this time, but you will the next time. Perhaps you were dutiful to your mother this week, but when your exams pile up, you'll forget your obligations to her. Shaytaan is unabating. You can be perfecting your deen, standing in the last third of the night, and still, he will find a way to seep into your veins.

He got a religious man to bow to him after committing zinna and murder. (Story of Barisa)

Imagine what we could do with a patience like that of Shaytaan. With willpower like that. With perseverance like that.

Imagine you came back to Allah that many times. You tried that hard. As hard as Shaytaan is trying to get you into Hell - you are trying twice as hard to get to Jannah.

So get there bi'ithnillah.

— — —

After the night journey of Prophet SAW, a lot of people were in disbelief. People who believed that he was the Prophet SAW and that Islam was the truth - had a hard time believing that he went to Jerusalem and the heavens and then came back all in one night. To this, Abu Bakr RA said:

"I believe him concerning the news of the heavens--that an angel descends to him from the heavens. How could I not believe he went to Jerusalem and came back in a short period of time--when these are on earth?"

You know, we believe wholeheartedly in Allah.

We believe in these "abstract" things called Paradise and Hell. We believe in Paradise having seven layers, and rivers, and jewels, and goblets that refill themselves. We believe in a Hell with it's blazing fire, the food of it being boiling pus, the bizarre punishments therein.

We also believe in the Day of Judgement. Where Allah will judge every soul - past, present, and future, rows and rows of people with their whole life in a book.

And we believe in angels constantly with us. Writing our every action.

These are all part of the "unseen". The things we believe but haven't seen (yet).

We believe in such "outlandish" things, but then when it comes to sabr, when it comes to patience, we fall short.

You believe that Allah will give you Jannah by His mercy - but it's hard to believe that He will give you things in this world?

What exactly can He not give you? The spouse you want? The career you want? The school you want? The car you want? The grades you want? The body you want? Which one of these things falls outside of His control? - Not a leaf falls without His knowledge. (Surah al-An'am)

Do you pray a whole night and then feel frustrated that He hasn't given you? Was the thahajjud too hard for you to continue to do? Was fasting every other day so painful that you gave it up after not seeing your duas immediately answered?

How easily you give up asking - how easily you become hopeless. One lost scholarship, one rejection, one mishap, and you yourself want to harden your heart to Allah. After you worked so hard to fill it with light.

You forget that He's the opener of doors. You forget how much reward you have in being patient. You forget that He is with the patient.

And let's say He doesn't give it to you. Let's say He doesn't give you a single dua you asked for. So what? Who are you to compel Allah? Who are you to question His wisdom?

He owns this earth and you're just a clump of dirt. He promised you Jannah, and you crave this earth's temporariness so much so that you'd sacrifice eternity?

If you can be patient for the hereafter, knowing His promise is true. You can also be patient here. On this earth that He has control over.

Hand over your worries, literally. Put your worries onto your cupped hands, raise them to Allah and give it to Him.

Breath. Wait. Al-Wahhab - the giver of gifts. He knows what to give you and when to give it.

Sabrun jameel. A beautiful patience.

friendships
and
family

"Your heart is like a feather in the wind - you may not have control over the heart, but you have control of the environment. Your aim is to settle the heart, don't let it sway without direction in whichever wind it finds." [Paraphrased from "Prophetic Musings" by Sh. Omar Suleiman]

It is absolutely, one-hundred percent, reality - you become like your friends.

You control the wind - you control the circles you chose to associate with. Growing up means losing certain friends. Either bring them with you to better imaan together (at least try really hard), or move on.

Try being with a crew of people who remind you of Allah, and you'll see the difference when you go back to the non-practicing crew.

This is not to say - don't be friends with less-practicing people.

This is to simply remind you and me - your friends are the wind that blows your heart. Surround yourself with good and you'll only see good. Surround yourself with bad, and shaytaan is only inches away.

Think about it - which of your friends is encouraging you to pray.

If you died amongst your friends - would they be begging you to say the shahada? And do you want to be resurrected with them?

Are you entering Jannah with them? Or are they dragging you to Jahannam? Or are you the friend everyone else is concerned about, the one whose slipping closer to the fire. Or are you the one who is pulling them to the gates of the garden?

— — —

Marriage IS NOT AN END GOAL.

It can be a means to the end goal - I shall remind you that the end goal is Jannah. But it's also not just something to check off a list, something to meet.

Have some actual goals in life.

You don't get a career so you can be stable and get married - get a career so you can change the fabric of society, get a career to change someone else's life, get a career to make money that you can use to build a school, an orphanage, start a pilot program in a third world country.

Learn skills: learn to cook, to roller blade, to paint, to put together furniture, to do immigration paperwork, to write poetry, to make candles, to hack a website, to write with your less dominant hand, to sing, to express, to empower. Learn things that make you feel alive.

To girls, it's beautiful if you want to be a homemaker - I think it's beyond stressful and if I could be half the mother my mom is, I'd feel accomplished. But if you're going to be a homemaker - be the best homemaker. The one with all the skills - from cooking to DIY to plumbing to carving wood into a headboard for your daughter's princess bed. Be that mother that wakes up for thahajjud, that brings breakfast in bed to their kids, that's hosting the cutest get together, that's active in all the PTA meetings, and every masjid event. Be the one that articulates stories with wonderment, that can inspire others, that knows world history like the back your hand; translating all the knowledge you have onto your children and your community.

To boys, there are other things in life that will grant you happiness, it doesn't have to come from a girl - nor mindless entertainment. Get some responsibility, do your laundry, try cooking, make your bed in the morning, stop playing video games three hours a day.

Make a list of things -

1) Spiritual Goals (Memorizing Quran, 1 juz, 2 juz, a few small surahs, a few big surahs, your favorite surahs. Learning the tafseer of every surah. Learning the differences in the fiqh issues, learning the intricacies of aqeedah. Thahajjud every day. Duha every day. Fasting once a week. Learning Arabic. Taking courses. Reading seerah. Knowing the names of the sahabas and their stories.)

2) Academic/Professional Goals (4.0s! - they exist! Publications. Promotions. Going above and beyond.)

3) Social/Relationship Goals (Parents, Siblings, talking to your baby

cousins, learning from your old aunties - and here ... this is where marriage fits in.)

Marriage can be so beautiful, and it can improve so much about you - spiritually, physically, and mentally.

But chill out. You are one individual, you belong to no one, you belong to Allah. What are you doing to please Him? What are you doing to make yourself a happy, content, cherished, valued person?

It doesn't all magically happen after you decide to put a ring on it.

There's more to life. There are scholars who didn't get married, too engrossed in their search for knowledge, too involved in loving Allah that they knew they wouldn't give their spouse the rights they deserved.

And you're not guaranteed marriage, nor are you guaranteed a good one.

All that you're guaranteed is a final destination, death, and facing Allah.

— — —

"You are not a child anymore; you are an adult, but for your parents, you are always going to be a child as we all know. No matter how old you are – 40, 50, 60 – in your their eyes, and they have every right to do this, you are always their little baby." - Sheikh Yasir Qadhi

We've grown up learning that heaven is at the feet of our mothers and we are told to treat our parents with the utmost perfection. As a child, it was kind of simple, we needed our parents for everything and we understood that saying please and being sweet and doing chores will get us what we want. And then we grow up and feel that we don't need them any longer. We make our own salaries, we buy our own food, we may dorm, we pay for our own phone bills, we buy our own clothes. But regardless of our independence, Allah gave them rights over us and we need to accept that.

Our parents can be difficult. Trust me - if you ask your parents truly they can tell you how difficult their parents were. Everyone's parents, even your parent's parents, have managed to stress them out. That's just the reality.

But how do we act with them? Especially when they anger us or when they stress us out or don't understand us. There's a culture barrier, a language barrier, a technological barrier between them and us.

Honestly, the best way to do this is to be their perfect child. In a practical manner - listen to them for a whole entire week. Smile all the time. And be super interested in everything they say. Engage with them in their stories and tell them about your stories. Tell them about your friends, and your assignments and homework and the new movies you want to watch. Become their best friend.

Your parents are the people who would starve themselves if it meant that you could have something to eat. They spent sleepless nights and countless working hours, just for you. They were there for you when you had no one. And they will always be there for you as long as they are alive. It's so scary to think, you raise a child and that child grows up to disobey you, to hurt you, to talk to you in a rude manner. It's such a scary thought that it is actually one of the signs that the Day of Judgement is near, a mother will give birth to her master - disobedience and disrespect will be widespread. And look around you - you already see that it is, all these shows and all these stories of children killing their own parents.

Bring your parents gifts - if you can buy yourself a new shirt every week or expensive gifts for your friend's birthday, you can for sure buy your parents a little something from the bargain store. Buy some groceries without being asked to do so. Clean the house while they're still asleep. Make them breakfast. And if you already do all these things - who said you couldn't do more?

Change your relationship with your parents. They are your door to Paradise AND your door to happiness in this world. They can seem backwards, they can seem so hard-headed, they can compare you to other kids, they can hurt you, they can force you to do things you hate. As long as they're not forcing you to obey them over Allah, they are only wanting what is best for you.

The only "weapon" against your parents - should be dua. Dua to make them more understanding, to make them see your points of view. And gosh the power of dua. Maybe Allah will give them a dream in their sleep and it'll be about you.

But seriously, become their best friend. On a personal note - My mom is literally my best friend, I'm still working on my relationship with my dad. But it wasn't always this way. It took months of me opening up to her, sitting in the kitchen while she cooked, making her come to my room and sitting next to her while she prayed. Talking to her about anything and everything. But after it all, there are no secrets between my mother and me. And my mother wasn't always the most understanding. She is very conservative in certain aspects and very cultural in others. I promise you - fix your relationship - it'll be REALLY awkward for a few weeks/months/years. But once you pass all that and can talk openly, it's like a total different world. They have wisdom beyond what we know.

For those of us blessed enough to have parents still alive, and what more - Muslim parents, we need to take advantage of it. And for those without - I pray Allah reunites you in Jannah.

— — —

One of the sayings of the Prophet is "The best among you is the one who treats his family the best".

We already understand that we should treat our parents the best. What about siblings? cousins? aunt? uncles?

I think that a lot of families, in NYC particularly, don't really spend time together. Everyone has different schedules and everyone has responsibilities and their own crew of friends. We would much rather spend our time eating out with friends or even chilling after class, than we would with our family. That's a problem.

We have this idea that our parents should be the ones bringing the family together and having family nights, or rather we think that Eid is good enough family time. But really, we, each one of us individually, have the power to bring family together.

We go through day to day with school and homework and sleep, and we say a word or two to our parents, and maybe annoy a sibling for a bit. But what about weekends, where some of us sleep in or make plans instead of being with our siblings/extended family. High school should be the easiest time for you to do that - many of us go away for college and then after that it's like career and life hits us in the face.

Girls - even more - I really hope I don't come off as sexist for pointing out reality but in desi culture particularly, girls get married off to another family, you will NOT get this precious time back where you could be spending with your family. It won't be the same.

And don't use the excuse that you don't have any siblings your age or cousins your age, you can hang with the little ones and have a lot of fun. Spending time doesn't mean opening up a Quran and being all religious. It means a lot of things - a movie, storytelling, board games, teaching them to cook or playing their made up games, asking them about their future, telling them how politics work or how college is or loans, telling them stories about your life, asking about their teachers and school dramas. Anything really. And with even younger ones you can wrestle or play hide and seek.

Stop closing your door and being on youtube, stop using homework as an excuse to just be alone on your laptop. Spend time with family - with siblings who annoy you - give them a pep talk, ask them about their life, make fun of silly things your parents do, make a skit.

If you're lucky enough to have a family - why not keep all the ties tightly knotted, you might be surprised at how much fun you could be having.

— — —

"You never know what you will wear first, the wedding garment or the shroud of death." - tumblr

This quote was referring to a discussion on Muslims who are still single and constantly anxious about marriage - who they'll marry and when they'll get married. Marriage is beautiful but at the same time it is responsibilities and compromises. Since perfection doesn't exist - you will never have anyone perfectly compatible in every way. So work on yourself first and Allah will make it happen when the time is right.

But we can take a lot from this quote even outside marriage.

Whatever we worry about - remember that death is the killer of all desires. So you don't actually know if you'll get that promotion, if you'll get that degree, if you'll buy that house.

When you get worried, saddened, or anxious about the future - think of death. Everything will become so miniscule - because what is ultimately important is your relationship with Allah and what you have to take with you to your grave.

There is a reason the Prophet (saw) recommended to go visit graves and remember death.

So forget the girl/boy in your dreams.

Are you ready to meet your Lord?

— — —

One of the things about being young is not having a ton of responsibilities. We go to school/college, come home, eat, pray, sleep. Some of us who work may not have so much time for enjoyment with friends, especially not with school and work and home.

But sometimes, we make a little more, we have a little more, and it's so tempting to spend this little more on a nice dinner and some new outfits. Well, I have a preposition: what if we handed some of that extra earned money to our parents or siblings. Or bought a random gift for someone in our family. I mean, we go all out for our friends birthdays, which is wonderful - but our families also have right over us.

So next time you have that extra few dollars, just buy some candy for the young one, or a food your mommy likes, or a new sweater for daddy. Or maybe just put it in an envelope and have it somewhere for next week's groceries.

It's these little rewards. The ones that make the people around us happy, and in turn, makes Allah happy. These are the little good deeds that can get us into Jannah inshaAllah.

— — —

"When you say salaam, it means more than peace be upon you -

the greeting means that you pray that Allah makes you have peace in every aspect of your life - financially, family, health school, everything. The people of Jannah get this greeting! Because that's where you will get real peace because in this world we will always have issues and problems and you can never get it. So that greeting is kind of like praying for them to have Jannah on earth." - Br. Mamunur Rayhan

This is actually profound in its own way.

My friend was saying just a few days ago that as beautiful as the greeting is - it has turned into a meaningless "hi". And that's true - so many of us don't even say it properly, we don't think of "peace" when we say it - we don't even think of Allah - let alone thinking "Oh Allah give peace to this person."

Sometimes, when random strangers give a salaam, it feels more genuine than an MSA buddy that says salaam.

We as Muslims pride ourselves in remembering Allah, remembering the akhira, more often than our non-muslim counterparts. And Allah gave us more than just the five prayers to remember Him.

We are to remember Him every time we see someone and depart from someone. He brings souls together, He created the bodies we see, made the bonds we have, placed us in these circumstances.

And we are always seeking this contentment, this peace - but we need to give it to others - we need to actually take two seconds of our life to give someone salaam and mean it.

The energy we let out is the energy we fill ourselves up with.

So even to those who you've yet to forgive, even to those who you have tension with, when you say your salaam, don't let it be fake. When you're faking smiles, at least let the salaam be real.

As real of you'd like the angels who come to take your soul to say salaam to you.

Those, whose lives are taken out by angels while they are pure, saying, 'Peace be upon you.' enter paradise for what you did. (Surah An-Nahl)

— — —

"Islam changed the idea that children are not possessions - they are a gift." - Sh. Mohamed Faqih

So parents have a say in our lives but at the same time they do not own us. We get to pick our career path. We get to decide whether or not to wear hijab. We get to pick what we eat. We get to pick how long we stay out. But it seems like, particularly in the desi community, we are property. We are shown off if we are smart, beautiful, handsome, pious. You hear it so often it is just fluff nowadays - "My daughter is studying medicine. My son got a full scholarship to this college. My son is memorizing Quran." And because of all of this type of bragging, our own parents sometimes feel the need to compare us. But we aren't materials or possessions for them to compare. We aren't rugs with stitching and embroidered designs for who has the most expensive or the most beautiful. It is our life. We have this right to live it in the way we decide. It is our career. It is our future. It is our soul and our deeds and our sins and our mistakes.

But before you start shouting "YAASS" we need to remember two things.

One is - our parents only want what is best for us. They don't want us to repeat their mistakes. They don't want us to go down a bad path. They are constantly worried about our health and our safety and our future.

And two - the second part of that quote. We are a gift to them. So act like it. Be a blessing in the house. It is so awkward at first - when you say things like "I love you" to your raging mother or your tough-love dad. But bring the warmth to your house. Remind them to pray. Give them little gems. Ask them about things you already know about just to give them the opportunity to advise you. Buy them gifts. Fold their clothes. Make them breakfast. Take them out. Hug them. Say good night.

Pray nafl just to ask Allah to protect them and preserve them and forgive them. Smile at them when they get mad. Make them melt. Make them feel like they created a perfect child. Get the most amazing grades you can and hand it to them with a sad face and say you failed. And then tell them it's a joke. Order pizza pies just as a surprise. Tell your mom not to cook for a day. Shine your father's shoes. Iron his thobe.

Your gates of Jannah are opened by their pleasure. So open them wider.

— — —

"He (Shaytaan) has lost all hope that he will ever be able to lead you astray in big things, so beware of following him in small things." - from Prophet Muhammad (saw) last khutbah.

Eid isn't justification for haraam. It isn't a time to forget the entire concept of lowering the gaze - brothers leaving Eid prayer and looking at everything that walks, and sister's flaunting about and trying to hide the fact that they're looking too. It isn't a time to forget gender barriers. It isn't a time to forget praying.

And we might be sinning without even knowing.

"the little things" like

1) Family drama - be grateful you have a family to have family drama - cause I swear there are people looking for just one relative, just one person they can call their own, because even broken families and fighting parents is better than no family at all.

2) Outfit - this is one of my pet peeves, when people don't like their outfit. Eid shouldn't be a competition of who buys the most gorgeous outfit. We should be thankful that we can even afford a new outfit! Wear your best, hands down, if you can afford it then go ahead and go all out - but make sure you don't make someone else feel bad about their clothes - and also make sure your heart isn't attached to your clothes - that you would be willing to spend that same amount of money on charity. I think it should be a new rule invented - for the amount you spend on your Eid outfit, give that same amount in charity. That is how you show Allah your gratitude.

3) The day itself was boring - why? Because you didn't engage in

146

certain haraam activities? Or because you don't have a huge fun family. Or because you don't have money? There are converts who don't get to celebrate Eid. There are also Muslims living in a country far away from any friends or family. Your own family members may not get a day off work for Eid to even relax. So you being bored is the least of Allah's concern. Go do something. If you have no one to spend it with then this is your turn to spend it with Allah. Stay at the Masjid. Or stay on your prayer rug in your nicest clothes. Memorize a new surah. Listen to a new lecture.

4) You didn't get off work/school - and that was the will of Allah. You have the privilege, ability, vigor and strength to do these things and Allah has also provided them for you. Wake up and smile, because you are the future. You make the future by the will of Allah. You are someone special.

There are 24 hours in this holiday. Spend every moment of it smiling. That's your sadaqa - the charity that will give you shade on the Day of Judgement.

— — —

I found out a friend of mine can't go home with cash. As in, by the end of the day, she has to get rid of all of her cash and change and find someone to give it to. And she chuckled as someone else mentioned this habit of hers and said, "no, I just like to travel light". It was cute. But it was more than cute. Even if it's a quarter, if this is that consistent deed, in the eyes of Allah it is greater than so much else.

And I came to think, SubhanAllah. The reason Allah made Jannah so big, so spacious. It's for people like this. With so much kindness and so much generosity and so humble that they think nothing of it.

And really, I'm amazed by my friends. And the deeds they don't brag about but I see.

A friend finishes Quran every month. Some of us are lucky if we even accomplish that during Ramadan. Some of us are squeezing in a juz a month. Some of us can barely do a page.

You might even have these friends with their secret deeds you don't know about. A friend that wakes up an hour before fajr, just to talk to

Allah. A friend that prays more than fifty rakats a day. A friend that reads a juz a day. A friend that memorizes a surah a month, a surah a week. A friend that sponsors an orphan. A friend that massages their parents feet. A friend that gives half their paycheck to charity. A friend that fasts three days a week.

Some of you guys were put into the habit of things like dhikr. When you were a child perhaps, by your parents or by Islamic school; they forced you to add some dhikr to your life, such as the dua before entering the bathroom, the dua when leaving the house, or saying ayatul kursi after every prayers. Now you do these things out of habit. These things raise you in rank in Jannah.

And sometimes I'm extremely jealous. I mean some of you have these things down like the back of your hand, entire long surahs memorized, dhikr just out of habit that you've been doing for years. My parents taught me the supplication upon waking up - but now as an adult, I discover that there's more than that in the morning - that you can do a billion things in the morning - like reading the last ten ayahs of Surah Al-Imran, or reciting surah al-ikhlaas 3x, or a bunch of other duas that are so simple to say but worth so many rewards. Four simple phrases, worth more than sitting on your prayer rug from morning to forenoon and then some, just worshiping Allah. (See hadith reported by Muslim, regarding our mother, Juwayriya.)

In a seminar, the Sheikh mentioned that friends in Jannah will be hanging out together but the one on the higher level has to come down to the lower level and visit their friend. Someone from the back blurted "OH MAN!" and we all giggled. But then the Sheikh remarked, "That's not a good outlook, it means you are aiming to be at the lower level."

And we do that. We're lucky if we even get to be in Jannah, but inshaAllah, if we're in, why not be at the highest levels.

We can see our friends and family and think, wow, their level in Jannah will surpass us. But Allah told us to compete in good deeds. Your small dhikr can surpass someone else's entire night of prayer. Your one fast can surpass someone else's $100 in donation. Compete in good deeds, make Allah smile, make yourself closer, and make the world better.

So race to [all that is] good. - Surah Al-Baqarah
Compete with each other in righteousness. - Surah Maidah

— — —

"Look at all of the families in the Quran - it is nothing utopian." - Suhaib Webb

Sometimes we think our family drama is insane. The levels it can go to - so much so that we have broken Eids, and drama over wedding invitations, and who didn't go see who at the hospital, and how the land back in the home country should be split.

Man, Aisha's own cousins went around spreading that she CHEATED on the PROPHET - and not cheated as in texted some guy, but accusing her of adultery. They said she had sex! With a man! That wasn't her husband! She is the wife of a prophet! The wife of THE prophet!

That is a serious rumor to be spread about like that.

And you're over here worrying about what someone's going to say since they saw you on the same cart as some boy or how your aunt is talking criticizing your attire choices.

There is not a single family that doesn't have drama. We are human beings - we make mistakes - we clash with other human beings - it is in our innate nature. We are made up of different personalities and different waves of thinking.

Now some families have it worse than others - there are cases of abuse, hushed hushed - and those shouldn't be hushed. They should not be silenced. Seek help.

But the usual drama - the usual gossip of aunties over tea and the loud tirades of uncles with paan - the cousins vs. cousins drama - it's normal. Accept it - and move forward.

Allah loves it when people reconcile - so reconcile. Forgive because if Allah can forgive people who spoke ill about Him and defiled His words and dishonoured His blessings by using them to sin - if He can forgive those people - who are you not to forgive your blood relative.

Don't be the reason that someone else's doors to Jannah get's closed. And don't let grudges, anger or pride be the reason your doors to Jannah get closed.

—— —— ——

"Marriage is not a magical solution that turns a person into a righteous person." -- Ustaadh Nouman Ali Khan

You cannot wait till marriage to change. You go into marriage as a whole human being and yes, marriage can support change and you can grow in your deen with marriage, but it isn't a magic button.

You don't all of a sudden become a hijabi after marriage. You don't all of a sudden pray five times after marriage. You don't all of a sudden lower your gaze and stop having friends the opposite gender as soon as you get married. If you're not used to qiyaam, it won't magically happen. You won't have a husband reading Quran to you every day if your own Quran is gathering dust right now.

1) You cannot possibly think that Allah will give you something you aren't striving to be as well. So if you're out in coed groups at hookah bars, know that your future spouse might be doing the same. You might not get the person who prays five times a day if you yourself aren't doing so either. And to my girls, it's beautiful when a brother is so modest and humble and he lowers his gaze - make sure that you're doing the same because the ayah was for you too.

2) Why would you wait for marriage to start pleasing God. Has he not given you enough as it is? What if you don't get married? What if you die? What if you marry someone who doesn't even want you to be pious? What if your future spouse doesn't care for prayer or for hijab?

3) You will not be judged with your husband/wife by your side. You are judged alone. You yourself are accountable for your deeds.

You might be lucky - Allah might bless you with something beautiful. A doorway to Jannah, a spouse that raises your children with gentle hands and imaan as strong as the pillars that hold the deen together. You just might get all of that. But you could also potentially get someone who disbelieves in their heart. Someone who abuses you physically and mentally and emotionally.

You be you. You be ready. You get close to God and beg for all that you want.

And for those of you who are already married - work together. Your dilemma of finding someone is over - now all you can do is go higher.

Imagine holding hands, wearing crowns of light for raising righteous children, robes unimaginable, and ascending higher and higher, the honeymoon phase never ending, butterflies and gushyness everywhere, like a vacation for the rest of your life.

— — —

"Even shirk cannot disqualify the respect and honor that is shown to parents." - Sh. Omar Suleiman | Marked for Greatness: Surah Maryam Part 2

Even if your parents are attempting to force you into disbelieving in Allah, you still show them respect.

But most of us, for those born into Islam of course, don't even respect our parents when they tell us to do good things.

They tell us to eat healthy or wake up early or clean our room or come home in a timely manner and we scoff. Allah isn't testing us the way He tests some converts, whose parents might force feed them haraam and force them not to fast during Ramadan and force them to pray to statues of Jesus.

It's crazy how much more importance we give to our friends - friends who come and go and don't actually physically take care of us when we are sick or give us a place to stay and constantly worry about us. These friends didn't take care of us when we were helpless.

We find it a burden to fulfill our parents requests, be it immigration paperwork, billing, emailing, calling up companies, dealing with finances and insurance, or cleaning, running errands. These things that really don't take an enormous amount of time are things we put off and see as a burden. But we can be with friends and do absolutely nothing productive for hours on end. We can watch tv mindlessly as forty minute episodes go by.

My Lord have mercy on them as they brought me up [when I was] small. The Dua from Surah Al-Israa that we might utter lackadaisically after our prayers (Rabbir hamhuma kama Rabbayani Sagheera) - but do we contemplate on what this actually means?

It's awkward mending the relationship with parents. But be to your parents the way you hope your children would be to you.

We all have to be better. Imagine the doors of Jannah closing because of one exasperated sigh you let out in front of your mother.

The mother whose painful contractions are immeasurable. And her sleepless nights uncountable.

——— ——— ———

I once sat in a wedding hall thinking about how many people missed Maghrib but also how many people prayed in some crevice.

And then how the person doing the wedding was saying a dua for the new couple but it wasn't silent in the hall, it wasn't even quiet, I couldn't even hear him over everyone else.

We really need to change our weddings. And it truly starts with you.

If it falls during a prayer time - incorporate it. Do the adhaan. Do a jamaat. Remind everyone.

If you're a girl, you make your mahr more reasonable. Discuss it with your parents before proposals even come. Force your parents.

You make it harder on those after you. People are constantly comparing. You be the different one. You be the one to say no. You put an end. You start the revolution.

Yes, it will be hard. Your parents might not agree. That's why you start earlier.

No one said change is easy. But our religion was sent to change. To make life easier. To make it less about comparisons and more about internal. Genuine. Happiness.

If it's hard for you, perfect. You get rewarded for your effort. And think of how easier it'll be for generations after you, even amongst your extended family.

Cause the rift guys. Do it.

And don't be scared to make changes to how you want to practice your deen - to enforce the gender separation barrier or the no instrumental music rulings - it's your life. Start the next chapter the way you want to. Be strange. You're a ghuraba after all.

— — —

"Their religiosity is independent of you." - Sh. Yaser Birjas□

For people who aren't married and imagine their potential spouse:

Your deen - is your deen. A spouse might improve it - or they might not. Your relationship with Allah depends on you - your prayers, your dhikr, your Quran.

When looking for a spouse - you cannot expect them to have qualities you don't have.

1) If you don't have 5 prayers down - do that first. Forget finding someone to better yourself, use an alarm clock, use an app, use your friends and fix yourself. I'm sure you expect your future children to have a fundamental pillar of Islam down - but you don't even have it down! 24 hours in a day, if you take 5 mins in each prayer (even though you shouldn't quicken it), it's still only 25 minutes. Allah gives you 24 hours, and you're too selfish and ungrateful to give back even half an hour?

2) This is more for sisters who dream about their husbands having amazing recitation voices: when was the last time you picked up the Quran and recited the words so the angels could hear you. Recited - not shyly, but loudly, feeling the words hit your heart.

3) "I don't want my wife to have any guy friends" okay cool, are you done hanging out with your coed groups too? & vice versa. But the thing is - are you really going to text "bye" to all your friends the opposite gender, the night before you wedding? Is that when you delete all the opposite gender off your facebook?

4) "I'm going to start practicing (hijaab/qiyaam/Quran/etc) after I get

married inshaAllah" - yeah? Says who? Is there some magic button the rest of the married couples missed out on? What if your significant other isn't okay with how you plan on practicing your deen - don't you think that if you want to become practicing and have someone who wants a practicing spouse - they too want someone who is *already* practicing?

5) "I want someone who cooks" - guess what. "Both genders should know how to cook because neither feminism or sexism is going to help you when you're hungry." - at least some basic items.

6) And for those of you who want that extra practicing person. How awesome it would be to have someone who pray thahajjud and duha and fasts on Mondays and Thursdays and reads Quran every single day. Well - be that person. Why should Allah gift you something, where is your relationship with Allah? & Just because you may end up with someone who is on point with their nawafil - does not mean that it will for sure rub off on you and you'll get it.

Since we're on the topic - their past is none of your business. Religiousness changes - people change. None of you came out of the womb practicing your deen. Everyone has flaws. What you look at is the present. You can't look at things that Allah already forgave. If you see someone whose pious now - why on earth would you expose a past sin - it means Allah took them in already. And if they're worthy of Allah's forgiveness - who are you to be judging?

We have to all get back on track. Get back into full gear. Become this unstoppable force of nature. Go to the step you're afraid of taking. Fajr on time - yes. Thahajjud every single day - yes. Duha during the day - yes. A page of Quran every day - yes. Just make a list and keep checking things off. You have no idea how far you can go. It is Allah who facilitates it for you.

At the end of the day - you face Allah alone.

Your pile of deeds are not split between you and your spouse. It is your pile. Your grave. Your life. Your questioning.

Jannah is yours - Allah talks to you directly in the Quran, to enter His garden. Just you.

— — —

"Everyone of you is a shepherd and is responsible for his flock."

Sometimes the hardest people to bring closer to Islam is your own family.

Even in already Muslim families - correction - especially in already Muslim families.

Take every opportunity you have to pull in the little ones in your family - to get them excited about Islam, to get them into the habit of praying.

You'll be surprised to find that your cousins who are of age - 16, 17, 18, 19, 21 - they aren't praying 5 times. And it's not to say that they are "bad" in any sense of the term. Maybe they just haven't realized the severity of the punishment for not praying, maybe they haven't understood the necessity for it, maybe they never found the sweetness in it.

Gentle words, playful words. Use them and help them and yeah, they may not listen. Yeah, they might roll their eyes. But at least when you face Allah, you can say you tried. And it's not you who guides, it's Allah who guides

You don't know what words will stay with your family members. Maybe they don't pray now. Maybe they won't pray now. But maybe when a hardship hits them, they'll hear the echoing remainder of your reminder to pray.

And of course prayer isn't the only thing - but it is a pillar. It is the foundation. It is the first thing that you're asked about.

"And remind for verily a reminder benefits the believer"

— — —

A story paraphrased from the Al Maghrib Class: The Prophet's Smile:

The Prophet Muhammad (PBUH) was wearing a ring once and a man approached him. The man started talking and the prophet was listening, and then he, the prophet, took off the ring he was wearing and put it in his pocket. Later on, someone asked him why he did this.

To which the prophet replied - I didn't want to be distracted while he was speaking.

In this case, he didn't want to fidget with his ring while someone was speaking to him. But so many of us, when people that we even love like our parents or spouses, are talking to us, we are talking while scrolling our phones. - Sh. Yaser Birjas

It's something we do without really meaning any harm in it at all. For our friends it's almost something we are all accustomed to. We talk without looking at each other - we talk while both of us are scrolling instagram and facebook. It doesn't feel like a big deal because it's part of the culture. No one seems offended by someone "multi-tasking" on their phone while having a conversation.

And it's not the entire anti-millennial-generation, obsessed with selfies and technology speel. It's not about not being connected - because we are in some ways even more connected with the lives of others.

It's about being completely present for people. About picking up on their emotions, showing sincere empathy, picking up on their cues. Noticing how many grey-white hairs your father has on his beard. Noticing your mom's worried expression trying to hide behind her fake smile as she asks you what you want for dinner. It's about noticing your friend is hungry by the way they're biting their lip and holding their tummy. It's noticing the small sigh after the statement they made, or the uncomfortable expression they made as someone walked by. Or the bag under their eyes getting deeper because they're not sleeping well. It's about giving people full undivided attention. It's about being equally as ecstatic of a little child as they show you their twentieth rainbow drawing.

You've already forgotten half the memes you liked three years ago, the vines you spent hours zooming through, the pictures you've tapped on instagram. All of technology is a blur to you. But you'll remember the moments you were present.

And you'll regret not being able to remember your parents expressions after they've passed away. Because you didn't look at them enough, you didn't give them your everything. And they didn't have snapchat to appear on your phone.

— — —

"Righteous people love righteous people - people like yourself. They will love you - with no idea why. Because it's from Allah. Because Allah loved you first, and then Jibreel loved you, and then the Angels loved you - and the people then love you. Not everyone. But people who love the sunnah will love you."

Ever found people like that? No idea why people love them so much. It's like everywhere you turn, you see people loving them.

Some of us have parents like that. Moms that no one can say a word of abuse about. Moms that seem to be loved by every other aunty in the neighborhood, even the non-muslim neighbors love them. Or a dad that people from all over call up for advice, that cousins from every side love.

Some of us have friends like that. Friends that literally, it seems like they have some sort of super power. They don't have "haters". They only have good things said about them.

And in school - you'll notice that when people who are like this graduate, people talk about them. How inspiring a sister was, how kind she was, how admirable a brother was, and how much everyone misses their presence.

Imagine how beautiful and humbling it would be to become that person. That the Lord of the universe loves you - that the highest ranking Angel, the one who carried the revelation, the one who was sent to so many prophets, the one who was sent to Maryam AS - that he loves you. And then, the righteous people in the world love you. You did nothing of benefit to them but they still love you.

May Allah make us one of these people. The person whom Al-Wadud, the eternally loving one, loves. Ameen.

"Live in such a way that if someone spoke badly of you, no one would believe it."

— — —

"If you are seeking the closeness to the Beloved, love everyone.

Whether in their presence or absence, see only their good. If you want to be as clear and refreshing as the breath of the morning breeze. Like the sun, have nothing but warmth and light for everyone." – Shaikh Abu Saeed Abil Kheir

There is a reason why we are told to make 72 excuses for our brothers and sisters. There's a fun game with that too - you're given a scenario and you have to make 72 excuses. (For example, scenario: a Muslim brother walks into a bar. Excuses: he needed change for a $20, he needed to make wudhu, he was looking for his friend, he owed money to someone inside, etc.)

It's not just about Allah being the best judge and you have no right to judge. It's about expressing your love. In their presence and in their absence. Because if all you give out is love, really, it means all you have is love.

People are filled with flaws, but it's up to Allah to judge them on their sins. All you are to do is to see their good. Think back to Prophet Yusuf's story, his own brothers tried to kill him, but years later, all he had for them was love and mercy.

When Allah can love even the very people who at some point denied His glory and His existence, what makes you, a mere human, any more special?

Blessed.

"We often think of poverty or the lack of worldly things, as a hardship and a test. We forget that pleasure and riches constitutes as the same kind of test."

Sometimes, I think this is probably the harder test. Because the one who is poor, it's "in his face" that he is poor. It is obvious to the individual that they are being tested and they must ask Allah for His provisions.

The one who is blessed, like the majority of us - with our overflowing wardrobes, myriad of food items, and technology - forget this test. We forget to be grateful.

And it's more than just saying that we are grateful - it's living by that humbleness and gratitude. So that things like train delays don't get to us - small things don't ruin our days because Alhamdulillah for all that we have. Let us all keep our blessings in mind next time the small things happen. Not because "it could've been worse" but because Allah testing us and we should pass this test.

— — —

"When we do a task and we think it's so easy, we have to remember - it's not easy because you're awesome, it's easy because Allah made it easy for you" - Ustaadh Nouman Ali Khan

I think that our levels of arrogance grows each day, it's terrible. We belittle classes because "oh, that was an easy A". We belittle our siblings because "back when I was doing fractions it was sooo easy". We belittle career paths because the only hard major is the premed field - right? [sarcasm]

To a certain degree, I think that's also one of the reasons people procrastinate. Because we've done it before, right? We've written 20 page papers in one night, or oh, it's an "easy" paper.

We need to constantly remind ourselves - Allah fashioned us. He gave us our intellects, He gave us our talents, He made it easy and He blessed us with the opportunities. We can't be conceited, because none of this is our own doing - if we even think that it is by our own willpower, then we are no better than Firaun.

May Allah protect us from ever having an ounce of arrogance - remember that Iblis turned into shaytaan for one sin and that sin was arrogance. And may Allah make all our obstacles easy for us.

— — —

"Some of us think that thauba (asking for forgiveness) is reserved for the month of Ramadan. Or that it's for only the sinners. Or that thauba is something that a person has to resort to after he/she has committed a sin." -- Sheikh Muiz Bukhary

Firstly, none of us are free from sin. It is in our very nature, as human beings, to sin. Except for Prophet Muhammad (SAW), all other prophets are KNOWN to have been sinners. But when Allah asks us to repent, He doesn't say "Oh sinners, repent", in the Quran it says "O you who have believed, repent to Allah with sincere repentance." (Surah At-Tahrim, 66:08)

Secondly, Ali ibn Talib, he was one of the ten that was PROMISED Jannah, yet he spent his entire night in prayer. What was it that made him do that if not the love of Allah?

Thirdly, even those promised Jannah, still sought repentance. For us, it's hard to imagine, our beloved prophets and the wives of these prophets and people like Maryam (as), what sins did they commit that they needed to seek repentance for? Yet they sought repentance.

We commit a bajillion sins without even being aware. You may not even realize you're sinning. In our society we see filth and don't lower our gaze because it's "the norm". We listen to music that sexually objectifies women and only talks about the pleasures of sex and drugs.

Some of us might swear, gossip, get mad at our parents. Some of us eat too much, gluttony is a sin after all. Even if you spent your entire day locked in your room, you may have seen an ad pop up on the side that may not be appropriate. Or perhaps a scene on a tv show that's "good for the storyline, I just close my eyes when they do stuff".

Why would Allah punish us then? For these sins, especially if they are hard to avoid for some of us.

Allah doesn't want to punish us. He wants to forgive us. Why do you think He's always telling us to repent? Why would He set all these guidelines of how to wash away bad deeds if He didn't want us to wash them off? Allah loves it when we go to Him.

We should seek repentance after every prayer. And then at night too, when we are in bed about to sleep, just try and remember things we may have done and make sure to ask Allah to forgive us for them, sincerely. Even if you feel like you didn't do anything wrong, you should ask for His forgiveness, because there's only good to come from seeking forgiveness.

— — —

"As Our ayahs came to you, and you had ignored them. In the same way, you will be ignored today." - Surah Taha, 20:126

Ouch. Can you imagine Allah forgetting us? What would happen to us if Allah forgot about us as often as we forget about Him? When we're hanging with our friends and we forget that it's prayer time. When we're busy zoned into a tv-show that we ignore our parents call, forgetting that Allah told us never to do that. If Allah forgot to feed us one day - cloth us, shelter us, keep us safe. What would become of us?

— — —

"If you don't even care about your own dua, how do you expect Allah to care?" - MD Hassan

It's like after every prayer when we spew haphazard Duas for our parents and our grades and Jannah.

But when was the last time you begged. Like a real beggar. Falling into sujood. Imagining His throne and talking to Him, pleading Him for something.

Quick Duas we memorized and think that'll fix our problems. But these Duas are made to facilitate conversation with Him. If you're just uttering some arabic terms you barely understand - are you really making Dua?

"The believers are fulfilled by the gift of Dua: calling upon Him comforts them." - Sh. Omar Suleiman | Surah Al-Ahqaf Tafseer

So beg the giver of gifts, Al Wahab & Al Wudud. Ask for His mercy and ask for His blessings. Ask for the well being of your future spouse. Ask for the highest possible grades. Ask for the protection of your friends.

But when you're asking, really care. Implore Him. Whether it's at the last third of the night on your prayer rug, or in rukoo' in the midst of a jamaat prayer. It's your connection with Allah.

He owns the world. He created the hearts. What do you want? What can He NOT give you?

— — —

"After being in a developing country, being crowded by child beggars asking for food, seeing the poor make temporary tents subject to the whims of the police or the government, I came back to my three bedroom home with a lawn. And my twelve year old self was overwhelmed by the abundance. [. . .] We always want more: flatter stomachs, softer hair, whiter sheets, more pixels on our tv screen. These are the things we want." - Professor Sunaina Chugani

In my master's class we were learning about consumption, loss aversion and hedonic adaptation. My professor was breaking down "Why do we want more?" All of us have enough - the fact that you are leisurely reading this - means that you have enough. You may struggle financially, but you are not poor.

She proposed three reasons:

1) To have a purpose: Because that really is people's goal in life. To get the dream house and dream car and the best makeup collection and the rolex watch. The materialistic things keep people going to work.

2) To be distracted: Because we can't be by ourselves. When we get alone, away from phones, tv and people, we find a certain sadness, a gaping emptiness. We don't like pure, unadulterated, reality. We don't want to think about death.

3) To cope with psychological insecurity: this is referring to the correlation between self esteem and materialism; very apparent in

middle school and high school children.

But see, there are things that combat this desire for more and for us, religion does that.

Islam gives us contentment. If we truly have gratitude, we feel happy with everything we have. We don't get caught up in the hampster wheel of consumption because we appreciate everything we already have. Because when you go to bed at night, you thank Him for the bed, the phone, the room, the home. When you take a sip of water, you thank Him for the sip.

You know that you are only in this position because Allah granted it to you. He could have tried you with poverty - especially with immigrant parents - just contemplate for a second on how different life would be if your parents stayed in the homeland. If they weren't rich in the homeland. If you grew up in a slum and didn't have the access to education like you do now.

Allah did not try you with poverty.

But He's trying you with wealth.

Are you passing? Or are you failing?

— — —

"You don't have to change the whole world. You just have to change YOUR world." - Br. Mamunur Rayhan

Sometimes the burden of the world seems heavy. It's upsetting to see injustices occur - to people around the world - to animals around the world.

And it's like we have absolutely no control, we are absolutely powerless.

And although that is true - for Allah is Al-Khaliq and Al-Malik. We do have control over some things.

For example, when I hear about certain horrifying things, when I see these videos that go around about young children in countries going through so much pain, I get deeply upset. But at the same time, I know that they are probably guaranteed Jannah. I mean, their trust in

Allah, their praying amongst rubble, their living on with perseverance with no family by their side - they die as martyrs. With belief etched into their hearts. Complete utter tawakkul. They have to be going to Jannah.

But me - with the countless blessings given to me - day in and day out. Shelter, food, provisions, education, clothing, family, the luxury of technology, the privilege of clean water - I still don't have that level of tawakkul. I don't have a guaranteed Jannah.

My world is different. My test is that of ease - with a sprinkles of hardships like health/family/finances/exams. But for the most part - you and me are tested with ease.

We can't change the whole world, but what does changing our world do?

Our world as in our habits - the outlook we have in life. Being grateful for the things we have and then using them well. Being charitable, being kind, staying silent when we have nothing good to say.

Our world can also mean our environment, our friends. Finding those that make us better, point out where we are slacking, push us to be higher in our deen.

Changing our world in a way does change the world around us. It changes our consumption habits, it changes our family relations, our friendships, our time management.

"Everyone thinks of changing the world, but no one thinks of changing himself." - Leo Tolstoy

Change starts with you.

"Indeed, Allah will not change the condition of a people until they change what is in themselves." - Surah Ar-Rad, 13:11

— — —

"Then you will be asked about all of the pleasures you enjoyed in the world"

It's okay to want material things. It's somewhat in our nature to want beautiful things for our homes or things to beautify ourselves like attire and jewelry, a beautiful car.

But when the desire for that leads you to feel jealous of other people or frustrated about your own financial condition or something along those lines, we need to take a step back.

Our ultimate goal is the pleasure of Allah. Once we take that into consideration, and keep that in our mind at all times, everything else is put into perspective.

What will these material things do for you on the Day you will meet your Lord?

— — —

Yesterday after isha, I sat on my prayer rug doing tasbeeh and noticed my bed and how pretty it was and said Alhamdulillah. And then I decided it would be kind of fun to say Alhamdulillah for every noticeable item in my room. So I let my eyes trail around the room, saying alhamdulillah at each thing I saw - my hand bags, my wardrobe, my curtains, my desk, my candle -

And then something happened when I came to my decorated graduation cap on my bookcase. I said Alhamdulillah but really meant it. Like, it reminded me of something so much more than a graduation cap - it reminded me to be so grateful to have gotten an education. Not just any old education, but a good one. Where I learned things. Had I lived in another circumstance, I may not have had the luxury of an education. Had I had a different set of parents, I may not have valued education. Had I had a different upbringing, I may not have even enjoyed learning.

And now I found myself glancing at things one by one and seeing so much more than the materialistic thing itself.

I saw the Harry Potter books on my bookcase and felt grateful for a really amazing childhood - free of worries. Never seeing the horrors children around the world see. Getting lost inside books, so much so that my mom would rip them from my hands so I would go to bed.

I saw the Quran on top and subhanAllah - not only did Allah give me

Islam when I never even actually asked for it - He gave me parents that taught me the Quran and then He gave me access to things that would make me fall in love with it. He instilled inside an actual attraction to the recitation of it, an obsession with tafseer, and He handed it to me.

I saw the dumbells on the floor and thanked Allah for my brothers who drive me crazy but life wouldn't be the same without them. They've calmed me down, they've supported me, they've made me laugh even when I was drowning in tears.

And it felt really nice. To stare at things and be reminded of so much more. To realize the gifts we don't take the time to thank Allah for. It's one thing to be grateful for a house, for a family, for deen. It's another to sit and see each thing - each memory, each story. Even small things, like the way lotion smells, or the fluffyness of pajama pants.

And I really want you guys to do it. Just sit on your rug and look around the room - pausing at each thing and seeing what it reminds you of.

— — —

"And my success is not but through Allah" - Surah Hud, 11:88

Sometimes, all the studying in the world doesn't give us the result we want. So study - study hard, but relax. Because success only comes from Allah. If you're meant to succeed, Allah will grant it to you tantamount to your efforts. And even when it seems that He didn't - it means He has something way better in mind.

And with that in mind, there's another side - sometimes we get wrapped up in things - the congratulations, the "mashaAllah's", the compliments. We forget that none of it would be possible without Allah. So stay humble - for He is the one who fashioned us from nothing.

— — —

At an internship, I was doing some cool stuff, sending some cool emails, using some cool digital marketing lingo. But I was thinking how it's an internship and not a job and how badly I wish I could work there with an actual career.

And then I was remembering how two months back, in every single prayer, after every adhaan, after every fast, whenever I was doing adhkar, I was asking Allah for this internship.

And I wouldn't know the jargon I know without the masters courses from last semester. And how I spent half of Ramadan asking Allah to give me an acceptance into the masters program.

And every single blessing - traces back to another blessing. Every dua, traces back to another dua.

And I keep asking for more things - and it's not wrong to keep asking, He loves being asked, that's why He sometimes delays things.

But we forget. Like the Arabic word for human "insaan" sharing root letters with "nisyaan" which means "forgetfullness". We naturally forget.

Which is good - in some ways. We forget our sorrows, we forget the pains people have inflicted on us, we forget our mistakes. But terrible in other ways - we forget our blessings.

So many duas were answered in your lifetime - even those silly little ones when you were a kid like "Allah let mom give me permission to sleepover" or "Allah don't let mom be mad about the test grade". And then the big ones - the academic accomplishments, the financial situations, the health issues, the family problems.

But we forget. And then when we don't get something - like Allah holds back on us just once - we deny His generosity. We say He's never answered us. We say He's never given.

Forget being thankful for the blessings we think we deserve - like our senses, intellect, family, clean water etc. We're not even thankful for the blessings we begged for.

Make it a rule - to pray two rakats whenever any of your duas get answered. And then maybe to write it down. Make a dua list - and star the ones that get answered. So one day, once a week, a month, or even once a year. You can look back and thank Allah for every gift He gave.

"Therefore remember Me, I will remember you, And be thankful to Me, and do not be ungrateful to Me." (Surah Al-Baqarah 2:152)

Alhamdulillah x infinity.

— — —

"So I went to the salesman and told him I wanted a pair of jeans and gave him my size. He asked me if I wanted slim-fit, easy-fit, or relaxed fit, you want button fly or zipper fly, you want stone-washed or acid-washed, do you want them distressed, do you want boot-cut or tapered, etc. My jaw dropped. I then said, I want the kind, that used to be, the only kind. He had no idea what that was. So I spent an hour, trying on all these jeans and I left the store with the best fitting jeans I ever had. I did better. All these choices made it possible for me to do better. But - I felt worse. Why? I wrote a whole book to try to explain this to myself. The reason is, that will all of these options available, my expectations about how good a pair of jeans should be went up. I had no particular expectations when they came in one type, but when they came in all these types, dammit - one of them should have been perfect." - Barry Schwartz: The Paradox of Choice

This is really from a ted talk related to marketing and consumption and the notion of choice and how sometimes - more choices means less satisfaction overall.

"The secret to happiness is low expectations."

We have too many options - so now, when the meat at the restaurant isn't "the perfect bite", we scoff. We vocalize our disappointment, even though that's not what the sunnah taught us to do. When the dress doesn't fit perfectly we let out a groan and start complaining about our body and throw it in the back of our wardrobe thinking what a waste of money, instead of being grateful for our wealth and our health.

We need to calm down. We need to slow down the world a bit and take things in and be utterly grateful. Limit your choices once in a while, fast and feel hunger, feel thirst. Leave your credit/debit card at home and stretch $20 for a whole week. Let go of some small luxuries, don't buy the coffee, don't buy the makeup that looks the same as all your other makeup, don't eat your fill.

And we also need to also lower our expectations of people. You can't even live up to your own expectations of who you could be, who you should be - and you want people to live up to your arbitrary concepts of who they are?

Limit your luxuries, lower your expectations, and savor the small things - like the specks of rain that touch your face, the flicker of the train lights, the smell of warmth emanating from your heater, the soft curve of your pillow, the lint on your sweater, the way ink comes out from your pen, the clarity of your phone screen, the softness of your lips, the sound of a hushed night, the smile of your sibling, the laughter of your friends.

falling for
Islam

صَدَقَ اللهُ الْعَظِيمُ

"Allah's plans are better than your dreams."

Sometimes we think we know what is right - we think a certain school or career is right for us, we think a certain person is right for us, we think an opportunity is right for us. We constantly act as if we know what is perfect, as if we know where we should be going.

But there's a reason Allah is the best of all planners. He has us perfectly placed. All that is good comes from Him and even difficulties and sadness comes from Him - so that we turn even closer towards Him.

Things will never go the way you want them to because we don't see beyond a certain time and space and scope of reality. Allah knows the overall everything of how our life should play out. The person you were three years ago isn't the same person you are now and it definitely won't be the same person you will be three years from now. Circumstances change, habits change, life changes. You change with it.

"Remember the one, I walk and He'll run."

— — —

"Who is the maker of fuzzy bunnies and unicorns? Al-Latif, the Gentle, the Kind"

Allah has 99 names, stop saying Allah. Call Him by the name you connect to.

— — —

"When will YOU be greater than a speaker?" – Ustaadh Wisam Sharieff

We put speakers on a pedestal. They're mashaAllah, extremely knowledgeable and their words to inspire us and help us.

But really, it's Allah's words that are to guide us - the speakers just make it easier for us to connect to these words or understand these words or they remind us of these words.

But a lot of these speakers started out just like us - some random kids going through school and drama. Many of them didn't go to Islamic school - they went to public school. They fell into traps of shaytaan. And a great number of them also have degrees from regular colleges just like ours. I bet some of them fell in teenage love or slipped into a bad crew of friends.

And if we met their families - I bet their wives and relatives would have a word or two to say about how "amazing" these speakers really are at home. They aren't sin free. They don't proclaim themselves to be sin free. They probably lose their temper - they don't really walk about saying "Allah is with the patient" all the time and I bet a million bucks they don't say sweet sweet words to all their kids all the time just because that was the sunnah of the prophet.

They're normal people - just with crazy amounts of knowledge and good speaking skills. And guess what - you guys can get that knowledge too. You don't need to go to Islamic school to get Islamic knowledge. You also don't need to give up your dreams of med school just because you also want to memorize the Quran or learn tafseer.

Allah made this religion the middle path - just as He also taught us to seek knowledge. So put the TV off if it's been on for the whole day. Get up early rather than sleeping half your day and waking up after noon. There is sooooo much to learn. SOO much to do.

— — —

So I've gotten messaged about "how do I get closer to Allah/ how do I feel pious", and I've always given the same kind of advice - pray thahajjud (which also means getting five daily prayers done on time - but I always just assume everyone has that) & then learn the tafseer of the surahs you already know because it's not a lot of effort, you already know the surahs, but you see them in a different light, and when you then use them in prayer, you actually slow down because you know what the ayah means and where it comes from and what it's referring to. It's no longer a strand of syllables, it's now tangible.

But I have to paraphrase a talk from Ustaadh Nouman Ali Khan, because this is the most concise advice I have ever heard:

"Three areas you need to set goals for and actually do:

1) Worship: Am I waking up for fajr on time, am I reading Quran at fajr? Youth, you can't accomplish anything in life if you go to sleep late and then wake up at ten for fajr.

2) Knowledge: It's separate from worship because some people study a lot of tafseer and know a lot of tajweed but don't even pay attention in salaah. What is that knowledge doing then? My recommendation is that at the end of the year you've:

a) Studied the Seerah, any book, read all of them, one per year;

b) Made substantial gains in Quran: memorize one surah or more per year - including reading it's tafseer and understanding the vocabulary, focus and get it right.

c) Memorize at least three or four duas: this is putting knowledge into practice, understanding the dua means you know what you are asking Him for.

3) Service: We don't have to do things under our own banner, good causes are good causes. Personally, I recommend Muslims to be part of good causes that are run by non muslims so they get to see that Muslims care too. So volunteer, help out, don't publicize it. It will make you a better human being. It will bring you closer to Allah.

We talk about changing the world, we can't even change your day yet."

And if that isn't the cold hard truth. How far we could go if we implemented this? - we'd have a surah memorized per year, we'd have a few duas, we'd know some ayahs in depth, we'd have been a part of charitable causes.

But for most of us - by the end of the year we probably only read the whole Quran once - aka during Ramadan - volunteered that one time with some friends and took some pictures, heard a billion lectures but remembered nothing, watched a whole lot of movies and tv, just did a lot of schoolwork, a sprinkle of all-nighters, tried some new restaurants, and chilled.

Which is all fine of course. Alhamdulillah that we had the privilege and luxury of doing all of that.

But what did we cash in for Jannah?

Because that beautiful place where happily ever afters and wild weed dreams come true - isn't free.

— — —

"You've been listening to speeches your whole life – what has changed?" – Ustaadh Nouman Ali Khan

Take a long hard look at yourself. It's about time you had a reality check.

Lecture after lecture. MSA Events and ICNA Conventions. Youtubes and Podcasts and Al Maghrib Courses. You have notes on your phone, notes written down, a collection of tweets and quotes.

You also remember the feelings. The moments in the event when your heart swelled up with a burning passion to worship Allah.

But what has changed? Check them off. Think seriously, how have you changed? Have you made Quran a part of your daily life? Have you made nafl part of you daily life? Have you actually attempted to fix your relationship with your parents? Have you cut off unnecessary opposite gender friends? Have you actually stopped dressing in a manner you know Allah is displeased with? Did you really end up breaking the haram relationship you felt guilty about during the lecture? Have you actually started waking up for fajr? Have you stopped cursing? Did you stop watching filth?

Think back to every lecture that inspired you. Euphoric at times. But if nothing has changed - what was the point? An ego boost to make you feel religious? Or was it just a chance to look at someone you have a crush on? Or so you can have something to post on instagram?

Who are you? Where have you come? Are you ready to be questioned for why you haven't changed? Cause the reminders, they came. Allah gave them to you. It was you who didn't do the changing. Because Allah does not change your condition unless you attempt to change it first.

What are you waiting for? Marriage, and you'll magically change? Ramadan, cause shaytaan will be locked up? Hajj, so you'll have a clean slate? Or when the angel of death is hovering above you.

— — —

"A much neglected Prophetic Sunna is to make others feel important and appreciated—behaving and dealing with such love, care and concern that they begin to feel they are one of the dearest people to you." - Mufti Muhammad ibn Adam al-Kawthari

We sometimes forget to make people feel special. Compliment them - random strangers even - it could make someone's day. Everyone has their own circle of close friends, but spread out a little. You should be able to befriend everyone. To listen to their stories, to pick up their cues. You shouldn't make anyone feel like you're unapproachable.

There are people who anyone can talk to. Born leaders really. Everyone thinks they are close to them. They make them feel so special, so wanted, so important. The Prophet (SAW) would be holding the hand of a child and listening to their story while walking all around town - as if that child was his best friend, as if that story was so crucial to the growth of the ummah. It was his compassion. It was just his nature. And man, if we could be like that.

— — —

"The less you desire of the world, the more room you will have in it to fill with the Beloved" -- Shaikh Abu Saeed Abil Kheir

The dunya was made to test us and of course we need to exist here and become the best of people - in our careers, our social lives, our intelligence. At the same time, have you noticed how we can become obsessive about the worldly things?

And social media just boosts this - we see friends traveling or buying new things or eating amazing foods and we think to ourselves, what are we doing? We want to do all those things but maybe don't have the time or the money to do so.

But God is our provider. He provides them and He provides us. Don't desire the worldly pleasures above desiring solitude and love of Allah.

Find your inner peace and your relationship with Him in the depths of the night or the breezes of the morning. Fill up the empty space in your heart, fill up your time with more than just filler-movies and tv reruns. The hosts of Paradise are waiting for you. Make sure you get there.

— — —

"Make dua for everyone who crosses your mind. Honor the guests of your heart."

If your best friend's name is not in your duas - is he/she really your best friend? I really believe in trading duas. In other people making dua for things you want because - literally - making dua in and of itself is ibadaah. It is worship. It is rewarding. Regardless of whether you get the dua answered or not, it's still added to your akhira bank.

And seriously. When you pray in jamaat. Do you ever say "Oh Allah, answer every single dua of every person that is bowing to you right now." Do you ever sit on a train and think "Allah guide everyone in this train to the truth - to your oneness, and the sweetness of worshipping you." Do you ever see someone you love and ask Allah to give them everything that they want. Do you ever hug someone and ask Allah to lessen all of their burdens?

I was hanging out with a group of friends one Friday and someone came up to us and said "Who's gonna make dua for my exam. I know she will" and pointed to me. So I asked which exam and I made sure to make dua right there on the spot and later after jummuah too.

You know why? Because I want an angel to make dua for me. I want the servant of Allah that literally doesn't sin - to ask Allah on my behalf. Because when I make dua for someone's exam, or family, or pain - I feel like when it's my turn, that dua comes back. The angel says, "May it be for you too."

Really. You have no idea the power of dua. So don't brush off other people's dua. When someone asks you to make dua for their orgo exam - just make the dua! Don't forget it! Don't just say inshaAllah and not act upon the verbal agreement you just made! Do it!

Make dua with specific names. A person comes to mind - a friend forgotten, a relative far away, a person you barely know - there's a reason the thought came to you. So make the dua. It's so small. But the power behind it, the angels that write it, the magnanimity of it, will one day be visible.

So dua it.

— — —

"Live your life as la ilaha illa Allah"

And constantly remember that we are all here for the same reason - to worship the One, the only, Allah. And our ultimate goal is to see Him.

Constantly think to ourselves - at what state do we want to die and meet Allah. Not just the moment of death, but who do you want to be WHEN you die. What kind of person do you want to be - be it now. What kind of friends do you want to have - have them now! How much Quran you want in your heart - make it now. Don't wait any longer. Don't wait for things to happen before you fix yourself and your environment.

— — —

"Every love that leads away from His love is in fact a punishment; only a love that leads to His love is a heartfelt and pure love." — Ibn Qayyim Al-Jawziyyah

So if loving entertainment means you hear lyrics in the middle of your salaah, or you're rushing prayer to go back to netflix, and in your salaah you remember a fictional character and the plotline of the show you're on - know that these things are only deterring you.

If loving your grades means you skip out on sunnah portions of prayer, or leave off prayer outside its due time because you're too busy "in the zone" studying - know that your grades mean nothing.

If the friends you love lead to you disregard your prayers, to go places you shouldn't go, to talk in a way that your angels have to scribble down the deeds of gossip and swearing - know that they aren't helping you to Jannah.

But if your love for grades leads you to tire your feet in qiyaam, if your love for your friends lead you to be talking about Jannah and Allah and sit in a room in the library in the middle of the week reading Quran together, if your love for someone pushes you to fast for their duas, if your love for someone props up in sujood and you ask for their well-being, protection, success, then know that you're getting somewhere. Bi'ithnillah.

Know that He's the one who blessed you, made it easy for you to do these deeds, and gave you the privilege of having these friends, and feeling this love.

— — —

"The religion will vanish with one sunnah at a time, just as a rope breaks one fiber at time." - Abdullah Ibn Muhairiz

And we see sunnahs being disregarded. First with the sunnah of prayers. Most people keep the sunnah of fajr (if they wake up on time) and the sunnah of Maghrib. But the hardest would probably be the sunnah of duhr and isha that most people tend to neglect.

There was a saying, "The sahabas would do a sunnah because it's a sunnah, and we leave it because it's a sunnah."

Not just sunnah for prayer, but other sunnahs like reading Surah Al-Kahf on Friday, putting on the right shoe first, the dua before leaving house, the dua for bathroom, drinking in three sips, sleeping on your right side, tasbeeh of the salaah, ayatul kursi after salaah, qiyaam-al-layl, Surah Al-ihklaas before sleeping, gift-giving, feeding people (even just friends) and more.

A speaker once said, you maintain your sunnahs because they protect your fard.

I'm sure there are sunnahs we all do - and so many more that we don't. But, if only we knew the reward for doing these things, we would drop things and do it.

This is the man who talked to Allah for your protection. This is the man who will be begging for you to get to Jannah on the Day of Judgement. The best to his wives, the best to his friends, the best to children, the best of the best. Even the secular world has to attest to his influence on mankind.

But as much as he loved us - do we love him? He prayed qiyaam until his legs hurt, all night just asking about us - the people who will believe after his era. And we can't even send salutations to him throughout our day. We can't even follow his example in worship.

Yet we want to sit in his garden in Paradise. And we dream of drinking water from his palm.

— — —

"There is no currency in the hereafter except for our deeds." -- Sheikh Saad Tasleem

The palace with the servants, the magnanimous amounts of food, the perfect body with changes in physical beauty depending upon whimsical desires. The adventures of worlds that belong to just you with equally beautiful friends and family. The never empty goblets of any and every kind of drink. Ornaments of diamonds and unheard treasures.

Can a world like that be free of charge?

So besides the mandatory prayers, what more have we done. How much have we put into our bank account for the Akhira? Because our sins have cost us debt - the swearing, the disobedience, the immodesty, the inappropriate gazing, the sins of premarital relationships, the gluttony, the vain speech, the backbiting, the white lies to our teachers or parents. With that much debt, from big sins to small sins, how much good have we even accumulated?

It's time to be wary, are our bank accounts empty or maybe they're still in the negatives. How much dhikr can we do to make up for the haraam that went into our ears? How many nafl prayers must we pray to make up for the footsteps we took to in the wrong path?

Think harder, try harder. For "Jannah isn't free."

— — —

"Verily your Lord is Generous and Shy. If His servant raises his hands to Him (in supplication) He becomes shy to return them empty" [Ahmad, Abu Dawood, Tirmidhi]

God is the only one who can give us what we want. Who can give us everything we want. So ask for the big things, the small things, for other people and for yourself. Ask for the most outrageous things, ask for the cliche things, ask for the bizarre things. The things you might even feel shy to ask Allah for - ask anyway. Things that seem like an impossibility - ask anyway.

Childish wishes on pennies thrown into fountains, or blowing out birthday candles and dandelion flowers and waiting to see the first star. You've got the Master, the Lord, the Creator. You talk to Him every day, 5 times or more. Thank Him for what you have - and ask for so much more.

He will never be tired of giving.

— — —

"If the world to Allah were equal to a mosquito's wing, then He would not allow the disbeliever to have a sip of water from it." [At-Tirmidhi]

"By Allah, this world is more insignificant in the eye of Allah as it (this dead lamb) is in your eye." [Muslim]

During summer break for many of us in NYC, I see posts all over social media of others exploring the world, doing study abroad and seeing such beautiful places, or going on vacations living in luxurious hotels. A part of me feels happy for them, and I also catch myself hoping to be able to do such things one day - and yet somehow I am reminded of these hadiths, over and over again.

The world is beautiful, yes. But it is completely insignificant in Allah's eyes. It's a stepping stone, it's a bridge, it's a million different analogies of temporary residence.

Over and over again in the Quran, we are reminded of this: "But the Hereafter is better and more lasting."

The doors of Jannah are open, Jannah with things beyond our imagination, a place where we don't pay mortgage and rent and airline tickets to see wondrous springs, Jannah with its rivers and fountains and extraordinary gatherings, Jannah with our beloved Prophets as our neighbors, Jannah with so much to offer - for those who believed.

Chase after it, beg for it, surely Allah loves the one who asks, even if you feel you don't deserve it - because none of us deserve Jannah, it is said that it is only by the mercy of Allah that we even get Jannah, so pray for it - surely, it's way better than anything on this world.

— — —

"A person cannot experience the taste of biryani or ice cream or know what it feels like to drive a car without doing it. WIthout trying it. You can't know the deen without experience it, without trying it." - Br. Mikaeel Olivieri

So many of us grew up with Islam and it's rituals. We hear this and think - yeah, I know it. I've experienced it. I do the praying and stuff. I read the Quran. It's kind of nice. It's sort of peaceful. I get it.

Except you don't.

Just as you have to actually eat biryani - and good biryani - to understand biryani and know it. Not the fake buffet biryani. And eating it after a day of fasting and swallowing it with mindfulness, not while watching tv and being distracted by your phone or gobbling it down. (praying while distracted, praying fast, praying with mumbled mistake-filled surahs is not experiencing salaah.)

Some of you know what the experience of deen means. It's not praying on time and praying slow and being calm. It's not reading Quran and swaying while listening to the smoothness and nuances of the verses pouring from your tongue. It's not the way the earth feels still when you fall to sujood in the last third of the night. It's not the coldness of the water that reaches your chest after a day of fasting.

Experiencing the deen is falling flat on your face, getting the wind knocked out of you, breathing out Allah, Allah, that's all there is. Allah, you're the only One I want to please. The only One I need to see. The only thing that matters is your happiness, my Lord, my Creator, my Perfect One, my Beloved.

It's not a collection of subhanAllah moments, miracles on exams, hardships disappearing into thin air.

Some of you know exactly the feeling, and you've felt it. Once upon a time, when you were on an imaan high, when you were going through Hell on earth, when you had your heart shattered, when you lost someone, when you got a rush. You know what it was, you know what it is, you need it back, you crave it.

And if you don't - I pray you do one day get that. That rush of insanity. Like I could die right now and see your beautiful face Allah because I swear that's all I need. It's overwhelming.

Chase it. Chase that emotion, chase that experience, you'll find a million small ones along the way - you'll find the drops of rain on your face as you make dua, you'll find the serenity of the last third of the night, you'll feel the angels around you, you'll feel your heart get brighter, your ears turn sensitive, your thoughts get cleaner, your burdens feel lighter.

If I could put into words what it feels to fall in love with Allah and Islam, I would. But I can't. I don't think anyone can. Sufi poets have tried. And even they can't. You have to find it to know it.

— — —

"Verily your Lord is the One modest and Generous, and when His servant raises his hands to Him in supplication, He is diffident (in some wordings, shy or hesitant or ashamed) from returning them empty." [Ahmad, Abu Dawud and at-Tirmidhi - Hasan]

Allah made you TO make dua and ask Him for everything. Who is going to give you if Allah doesn't?

We get five daily prayers to make dua, although we can be making dua around the clock, we do sit down after salaat to make dua. Sometimes we just say a quick dua, ya Allah forgive me, and then maybe if it's finals week or we want something at that moment, we'll add it, if we remember of course.

Notice how at times when we need Him - before an interview for a job, before semester grades come up, or when we want something materialistic - we can make dua really hard. Once that time frame is over, or once we get what we want, sometimes we thank Him, and then we forget that He gave it to us. We forget about the extra hard dua. That's why many times Allah delays answering our dua, because He loves it when we are asking, and if He always handed everything, we wouldn't even ask.

So keep making dua, there's always things to make dua for - selfish things are fine too - to Allah you CAN be selfish, you CAN ask for materialistic things and for dashing good looks and a drop-dead-gorgeous spouse and Jannah obviously. You can also be selfless, ask to help specific friends - say their names and how Allah should help them, make dua for people who have hurt you, make dua for people who have helped you, your family members, your doctors, your teachers, make dua Allah guides them all to the right path. Make dua for your future, for your future children, for your parents and grandparents. For everyone suffering. Just sit down after isha, you're not in a rush, you're just going to lay in bed and scroll through facebook or instagram anyway, so just sit down, just make dua, all the things you could possibly want for yourself and for others.

Also, for Ramadan prep, make a list of dua's, a whole page filled with them about everything you want - specific things, and things for other people of course. And during those sacred nights, you'll have a whole list to pray for.

— — —

"Stop waiting for Friday, for summer, for a boy/girl to fall in love with you. Happiness is achieved when you stop waiting for it and make something of the moment you're in right now."

You're not guaranteed another Friday, another summer, and marriage. You only have now. And the only guarantee is death. Happiness is a transient state.

Contentment. That's what you'll find. Once you start walking to Allah, you'll see how quickly He comes to you.

You'll smile when you're in sujood. And you won't be able to help yourself but say, I love you, I love you, Allah, I love you.

And when people ask how you're doing, with your insane schedule, your midterms, your dilemmas, your crazy life - you'll say, perfect. My life is perfect, Alhamdulillah.

Which of the favors of your Lord will you deny? When He gave you the best favor or all: imaan.

— — —

184

"The more you study [Islam], the more unattracted you become to the things of the dunya." Imam Siraj Wahaj

For some of us, it's hard to imagine a life without netflix, without music, without hookah, without coed groups. But once you realize how limited your time is - how the angel of death has your name on a list that could be crossed out any minute. How you won't be able to take your laughter, your books, your bed, your home, your academic credentials with you.

You realize, all there is to do is bow. You've got the fard rakats down, the sunnah rakats down, the nafl rakats down, and then discover the world of qiyam, thahajjud, duha, ishraq, awabeen.

You get all of that done, and realize still, that if Allah told the Prophet that He wiped clean the sins that were breaking his back, how much sin do we carry?

So become the one obsessed, with every curve in the book Allah sent, the familiarity of your prayer rug, and the taste of your tongue as you utter His praise.

For this world is a delusion, and we need to get home, Allah has so much more in store for us, if only we could see.

— — —

Alhamdulillah that He lets people forget.

So when you catch yourself remembering an embarrassing memory, thank Allah because He probably made everyone forget that incident.

Alhamdulillah for imperfect memories.

The only reason why we can continue to be close to family and friends who have done us wrong. Because we have forgiven, and we have forgotten, just as they have forgiven, and they have forgotten.

Alhamdulillah for strong memories.

When scents remind us of moments and people we've long distanced. When a word reminds us of a whole book.

When we can close our eyes and see the page of Quran we are

working on memorizing. When we remember the scribbles on our flashcard just in time to finish the final.

Alhamdulillah for faulty memories.

So we can write memoirs that aren't entirely true, and read memoirs with perfect embellishments. And see people in good light forgetting their flaws. Remembering only the good that they've done.

Alhamdulillah for not forgetting.

The sins we did. The sins we do. That remind us of our human-ness and need for the mercy and blessings of Allah.

Alhamdulillah for balance.

How beautiful is He, Allah. And how beautifully did He create our minds.

— — —

"This dunya is nothing but heartbreaks and heartaches; pack your suitcase and prepare for the akhirah. Keep it moving, this isn't your final destination."

You will never get what you want. Face that now. Accept it now. Because what you want is constantly changing, constantly evolving, constantly different. What you wanted as a child, what you wanted last year, what you want today, it's all different. And you've gotten things - you've gotten duas answered, pains taken away, materialistic gifts received, grades and peace and solutions.

But you will never get what you truly want in this world. All the money in the world - and still you won't get what you want.

Because what you want is to meet Allah. That's what you really want.

Jannah - that's just to explain that all your wishes will come true- your insane fantasies, the adornments, the luxury brand bags and watches, the wonderful cars, the gluttonous feasts, the wine and weed, the men and women of your pleasing, sunsets and sunrises and gardens and palaces.

Your final destination is more than that. It's sipping tea with your entire family, it's jumping on a full feather down bed with your best friend, it's sitting with the prophets, all of them, laughing your heart out at their jokes, it's seeing Aisha ra. hold Prophet Muhammad's (saw) hand. It's listening to your young grandparents tell you embarrassing stories of your mother. It's asking for rain and singing with Fatima RA, as it pours. It's getting talking to Adam AS, to Yusuf AS, to Ibraheem AS, asking him about building the Kaaba. It's seeing all the parents holding their crowns of light because their children were huffadh. It's seeing your parents actually show affection, with no signs of stress, no wrinkles, no worries. It's learning from your great-great grandchildren about how much technology changed when they were in the dunya.

It's sitting under His throne, asking Him all your confusing aqeedah questions, it's hearing Him welcome you with the word, salaam.

Do your part in this world, but don't plan on staying too long.

And whenever you're disheartened, whenever you are sad, remember the final destination, remember His mercy, and remember His promise.

"This life is a bridge, don't build upon it but cross over it."

— — —

Surah Ar-Rahman starts with perhaps one of the most popular and often mentioned names of Allah and ends with the verse: Blessed is the name of your Lord, Owner of Majesty and Honor.

So if your Lord is the one who holds that name, the blessed name, stop caring about what others think.

If you yourself know that you are doing your best. If you know that Ar-Rahman is watching you.

Don't fear the creation, don't feel the need to answer to the creation, you only answer to One, and He laid out all His names.

So you answer to the Merciful One, the Compassionate One, the Exceedingly Loving One, the Guiding One, the Gentle One.

You only answer to Him. Fix your relationship with Him, be happy with Him, fall in love with Him. Everything else is secondary.

— — —

"The most beautiful names belong to Allah: so call on Him by them." (Surah Al-A'raf, 7:180)

Often times we search for worldly ways to relieve our troubles. And yes, we need to seek out actual practical solutions - that is why you can't simply be sick and just pray to God it gets better but not go see a doctor.

But don't only see the doctor. You need to ask Allah to cure you too.

In the same way - any problem you have - seek Allah's help while also doing your part. And the best way to do it is to find which name you should call Him by.

You need a job - ask Ar-Razzaq, the provider, to provide you with a job that provides to all your financial needs.

You want to lose weight or get rid of your pimples - ask Al-Musawwir, the fashion of forms, to fashion you in the way you see beauty.

You want good grades - ask Al-Wahhab, the Bestower, to bestow upon you the good grades.

You want something done quicker - ask Al-Muqaddim, the Expediter, to bring it forward.

You want the truth about something- ask Ash-Shaheed, the Witness, to reveal reality.

For everything you want - there is a name you can call Allah by.

Find the name, ask Him, in the third of the night or in the rain. Find your duas answered.

— — —

"Everything besides Allah is disposable. If you lose anything else in life, then you can replace it with something. But if you lose Allah, you lose everything including yourself." - Inspiration 2 Series by Omar

Only those who have been there can truly know this feeling. Only those of you who were there or fell there accidentally and had to come back to Allah will actually know the meaning behind this.

The feelings of lost and loneliness and being scared and being sad with no idea why. Surrounded by friends but feeling like there's no one that's truly your friend. Surrounded by luxuries but feeling like you're suffocated. Everyone in the world seems to think you have a perfect life, but you still cried in bed for no reason. You couldn't pin point why. There was an emptiness in your heart. You filled it with so many things - boyfriend/girlfriend, smoking hookah all night, blasting music, excessively socializing, being gluttonous. Whatever you found, you put into your heart just to see if it would fill up and stop feeling so darn empty.

Until the day you discovered Him again. Again. And. Again.

And everything became clear.

And you found yourself. After you found Allah.

And sometimes, some people fall back and have to rediscover Him again. But if you found Him. Don't let go. It's not worth letting go. And if you've always had Him, you're blessed. You weren't given that test. Because the test of faith might be the scariest and the easiest to fail.

— — —

"Iblis had the knowledge. He believed. He saw Allah's dominion and all that He had created in heaven. Iblis's downfall shows that KNOWLEDGE ISN'T ENOUGH. You can study all the Quran and Hadith you want. It isn't enough." - MD Hasan

Sometimes, these lectures, these tafseers, the stories, the hadiths, and verses - they go over our heads. We hear, we believe, we say "yes, inshaAllah I will do so". But a few hours later, sometimes a few days/ weeks/months, we forget, we lose whatever imaan high we got, we take "a break".

We can take in all the information, sitting seminar after seminar, watching youtube lectures, reading books and books. But if we aren't doing the added things (after of course doing the fard), then are we really taking anything in?

What prayers can you add in? What fasts can you add in? What did you study, what did you write down, what did you read, and what did you change.

So many posts about taking advantage of dhul hijjah - the ten best days of the year - better than Ramadan. But you liked the posts about fasting, and you liked the posts about increase in dhikr. Where is that fast? Where are those dhikrs? Was posting it on facebook and liking posts about it sufficient? Where is the added good deeds on these days - or is the timing of Allah just horrible? You have work and classes and papers to write -- why are the best days now - Shaytaan isn't even locked up, how are you supposed to fast when it's not Ramadan, how are you supposed to pray Qiyaam, when are you supposed to find the time to read Quran. Your friends and family aren't doing iftaar with you - people around you are drinking coffee, people around you aren't praying at night like they do in Ramadan. It's not the "season" of worshipping Allah.

But then, are you really worshipping because you love Him? Or is it because it's a fad, because others around you do it, because it's the instagram thing to do.

Who is He to you? Is He your Lord, or simply the one you turn to only when you feel you need Him.

— — —

"He used to say, there is nothing more harder upon me in life, than when I was asked a question about halal or haraam; is this permissible or not. Because I am presenting the hukm, the ruling of Allah Himself. The Creator of the world." -- Life of the Four Imams: Story of Imam Malik

The Imam of the Maliki madhab, was nervous in answering these questions. A hafidh, a young boy who studied under Abu Hanifa, the Imam of the Hanafi madhab. I mean, this man had knowledge upon knowledge. And he was hesitant to answer these types of questions.

But we, with our limited Arabic, our google sheikh, our translations of the Quran, our chainless-hadiths, we openly, loudly, proclaim things as haraam and halaal.

If something seems to fall into the circle of haraam-ness, stay away from it. If you have doubt, just stay away. But there is no reason to proclaim that certain thing as haraam or halaal.

And using our own logical vices is fine and dandy, for personal intellectual satisfaction, but not for preaching a ruling onto another person.

We should be much more humble. The knowledgeable one knows nothing. You know nothing. I know nothing.

Seek the answers in the right places - when you don't know the answer, say Allahu A'lam. Don't try to come up with a ruling from the slither of knowledge that you have.

Have some patience, have some restrictions, have some humility, have some respect for people who dedicate their entire lives to this study.

And use the technology Allah gave you. There was a time where it felt like we didn't have access to sheikhs. But now we do - there's email, there's phone (there are numbers you can text anonymously to get answers), there's events, there's q&a sessions, sometimes even twitter (or Imam Suhaib Webb does snapchat).

And remember - although we live in a world of information overload and instant gratification, not everything is on the internet. There are tons of hadiths, tons of exegesis, tons of narrations and books that aren't translated nicely in modern English and posted as a pdf. There's a world out there we don't know.

We need to sit down. We need to study, to learn, to explore, to be proved wrong, to be reprimanded, to be taught.

This religion teaches discipline. You get that from your five daily prayers. There's also discipline in knowledge. And knowing that you know nothing, and that Allah holds all knowledge, the seen and the unseen. And you should only seek the knowledge for His happiness, for enriching your relationship with Him, and for benefiting your akhira. Not to be right. Not to give lectures. Not to give out rulings.

But do seek the knowledge, it has a haqq upon you.

— — —

"If it was about knowledge - Iblis [Shaytaan] would be the most honored because he knows the most. It's about what you do with that knowledge." - Dr. Farhan Abdul Azeez

Some of you were blessed enough with parents that could afford and wanted to send you to Private Islamic Schools. As bad as a reputation they may have in terms of their academic credentials - they still taught you deen. You memorized surahs, you were given Arabic class, and you were taught Islamic studies.

You know where the rest of us had to learn these things? On the internet. By ourselves. After we grew up and the ability of our memory to soak up ayahs deteriorated - that's when we started memorizing surahs outside the last juz. The stories of Ibraheem and Yusuf may have been told to us when we were children but the ones of Salih, Zakariya, Idris - even parts of the seerah - we had to willingly find that information.

You have piles of knowledge inside you and that's both a privilege and a responsibility.

This privilege of knowledge means that you need to act upon the things you know. If you know that fasting on Ashura deletes sins of the previous year, you should fast. If you know that the first thing you will be questioned about is your five daily prayers, you should pray. If you know watching a girl dance with gyrating motions in a crowd of men is wrong (ex:bollywood), you wouldn't watch it. If you know that cursing is a sin and abuses a blessing Allah gave you, you wouldn't curse.

Greater knowledge also means greater humility because you know that you are a slave and you know that there will always be someone more knowledgeable.

And it's your responsibility to share it as well - any little amount it may be - it's your torch in the darkness, so help someone else see. Be it a best friend, a sibling, a parents, or a cousin.

— — —

"We know what kind of underwear Michael Jordan has on but we don't know what the things Rasul Allah [saw] used to do." Sh. Abdul Bary Yahya

You know exactly where Kim K bought her wedding dress or the name of her child. All the NBA players names and high scores. When Katrina Kaif's next movie is coming out. Or who is dating who in Bollywood/Hollywood.

But think about how much we know of the beloved Prophet (saw). Do we even know his full real name? His nickname? What age he died? His mother's name? His favorite phrases? How he dressed? His habits (which are our Sunnah's).

And this is the man who Allah gave as an example. We should be ashamed we don't know the Seerah, that we don't know the names and stories of each and every companion and we don't know every which way that the Prophet (saw) lived his life. There is a world of knowledge to dive into. There's always more and more knowledge to gain.

How many of you guys know the Prophets (saw) life story by heart?

— — —

"Once you've tasted paradise, you can't go back. And the paradise of this life is in the worship of Allah"

There's this feeling. It's not the same as an "imaan high" that you get after a good lecture. It's not that streak of goodness you go on. It's so much more.

It's completely different. It's this awareness that Allah created you for this purpose - the worship of Him. And nothing else seems important anymore.

It's more than the taste of sweetness in prayer - though that is part of it. But once you reach this feeling, you will chase after it your whole life.

It's the wave of love you get after a night of praying, it smells like Ramadan walks after taraweeh, like breathing again after being sick for so long. It's better than butterflies in your tummy and giddy smiles.

Where do we find that feeling in anything other than the worship of Allah? Beg for it, and it'll come. Allah will run to you, all you have to do is try.

— — —

Allah answers the call of the one praying in the last third of the night. [Bukhari]

Allah answers the call of the one breaking their fast. [Ahmad, Tirmidhi]

Allah answers the call of the one calling between the adhaan and the iqaama. [Ahmad, Abu Dawud, Tirmidhi]

Allah answers the call of the one suffering injustice. [Bukhari, Muslim]

Allah answers the call at the end of every mandatory prayer. [Tirmidhi]

Allah answers the call of the one calling in the rain. [Abu Dawud]

Allah answers the call of the caller. [Quran, Surah Al-Baqarah]

Allah has to answer you.

You have a wishlist, a heart full of worries, a pinterest of dreams, big exams, and the desires of those closest to you. What do you want badly. How bad do you want it? What do the people you love want? If you don't crave something for yourself, then crave something for someone else.

— — —

"Dua is the entirety of worship because a person making dua implicitly believes 1) in Allah the unseen 2) that Allah is near to him 3) he feels impoverished and begs." - Ustaadh Mohammad Elshinawy

The fact that you make dua affirms that you believe in Allah. You believe that He hears you, even though you aren't raising your voice.

You believe that He cares about your request. You believe that He has the power to answer your dua, even if it seems absurd on a subjective - perhaps even on an objective - level.

But I remember making quick duas when I was young, it was like right after prayer you just really quickly say a "rabbana" dua you memorized, and say something like "bless my parents and give me Jannah, thank you" and fold the prayer rug in high speed before going back to the tv.

But then those serious times of hardship - when you need something desperately, when sickness comes creeping into your family, or after a death, or the pains in mending a relationship with your parents - at those moments, your prayers were slower, your duas were longer.

The thing is - if you're only slowing down your prayer and making duas only during hardship, you're missing out all the other times.

Because duas when you're happy are something else. When you can't stop sobbing in sujood because Allah blessed you with incredible people, when you can't help but whimper because He blessed you with this religion, when you can't stop smiling-and-tearing-together because He keeps answering every single dua, every single wish. And He gives you every single thing you ask for.

When you can't stop saying, I love you. I love you.

That's a whole different ball game of duas. It's a whole different feeling. But the only way you'll get there is if you never stop asking.

Always make your sujood the longest - just stay there, humbled. Ask for everything you want, for your friends, for your family, for the person you love. Ask for every stupid tiny grade, every silly materialistic wish, every future dream - the spouse, the house, the kids, the career. You won't be able to get up from that sujood if you really, really asked for things.

And if you're blessed and feel like you have nothing to ask for - just stay there thanking Him, counting it up, thank Him one thing at a time, thank Him for your intellect, your hair, your voice, your finger, every vein, every cell, every atom that makes up someone as stunning as you.

We don't need 11:11, shooting stars, dandelions, pennies in fountains. We have sujood, we have thahajjud, we have iftaar, we have rain.

— — —

"The secret of change is to focus all of your energy, not on fighting the old, but on building the new." - Socrates

It's not about the old you who was "bad" and needs to become "good".

It's you building this new person. This new amazing identity. This person who is different, with longer sujood, with better manners, with a more optimistic look of things, with a brighter smile. This person who makes time for friends, for parents, for siblings.

This person who makes sure to touch the book of Allah at least once during their day. This person who remembers others in their dua. This person who is happy with their body. This person who feels protected, taken care of by Allah.

As if you can almost feel Allah covering you with angels, writing, scribbling, their ink never stopping - not writing fast enough to keep up with your good deeds.

The new you.

And every day is a day where Allah gives you back your soul to start again. Be new again. Be His again.

37010697R00112

Printed in Poland
by Amazon Fulfillment
Poland Sp. z o.o., Wrocław